MINORITIES
and
the
POLICE

CONFRONTATION IN
AMERICA

by David H. Bayley
and Harold Mendelsohn
UNIVERSITY OF DENVER

Fp *The Free Press, New York*
COLLIER-MACMILLAN LIMITED, LONDON

Library of Congress Catalog Card Number: 69-12119
printing number
2 3 4 5 6 7 8 9 10

Preface

The purpose of this book is to explore the texture of relations between the police and the community, especially minority groups. In the welter of emotion that surrounds this subject, facts are at a premium. We shall attempt to provide an accurate description of the nature of the relationship upon which can be founded an analysis of the reasons producing strain and suspicion.

Implicit within the strategy of this study is the notion that relations between the police and the community cannot be understood unless the constraints on both sides are thoroughly explored. It is not enough to know that policemen are sometimes rude and overbearing or that minority individuals are distrustful of authority and sensitive to fancied slights. In order to understand interaction, one must understand the perspectives, attitudes, experiences, responsibilities, and emotions that participants on both sides bring to encounters. This study will not attempt to characterize the relations between police and minorities from the point of view of a detached observer. Rather, it will show how police and minorities perceive the relationship, for it is mutual

perceptions that make for the social reality with which
policy-makers must deal. Furthermore, the study will attempt to show what factors cause participants to approach
one another in a particular way. In short, by understanding
the world of the policeman and the world of the citizen,
especially of the minority citizen, it should be possible to
understand why interaction on the border between these
worlds has assumed the character it has.

The empirical data for the study were collected in one
American City—Denver, Colorado. We believe that relations
between the police and the community in Denver are not
unique. They do not have a logic that is dissimilar from
that in New York, Detroit, Philadelphia, or Atlanta. American culture is sufficiently homogeneous and its social problems, particularly, sufficiently similar throughout the country
that insights developed about police-community relations in
one metropolitan area are very likely to be applicable in
others. An explicit attempt has been made to use the
Denver data to suggest patterns of association that transcend
a specific context of time and place. It will remain for other
scholars in other cities to determine whether our hypotheses
are in fact generalizable.

Denver is the twenty-third largest city in the United
States. In 1966, when the study was made, it had a population of 521,896.[1] The greater metropolitan area has a
population in excess of one million. There are two primary
minority groups, evaluated in terms of numbers and problems
of accommodation with the majority community: Negroes
and persons of Mexican-American extraction. Twelve percent of the population is Spanish-named and 9.5% is Negro.
There are also Jews and some American Indians in the

[1] This figure was furnished by the Denver Planning Commission.

community, but they do not present serious problems for police-community relations. For purposes of analysis, Denver's population will be treated as three distinct ethnic groups: Dominants, who are whites of non-Mexican-American extraction; Negroes; and the Spanish-named.

It should be understood that these divisions within the community are a result of a combination of cultural and racial factors that create feelings of social difference and group identity. People of Mexican-American heritage, while tending to be Latin in appearance, have in common the Spanish language, an historical tradition, and a sense of cultural uniqueness. Negroes participate to a greater extent than the Spanish-named in the culture of America; they do not, for example, speak a different language, but have a more distinctive physical appearance which sets them apart. The majority community is composed of everyone else, people who are neither Negro nor participants in Spanish culture. We have chosen to designate these groups as Dominants, Negroes, and the Spanish-named. These labels are both descriptively accurate and unencumbered with emotional connotations.

As of the spring 1968, Denver had not been the scene of a minority riot. Although once or twice a riot was imminent, the city has been spared the full fury of urban discontent. This circumstance is indicative of the fact that relations among ethnic groups in Denver are better than in large urban areas of the East and Midwest. This is cause for congratulation, but, as we shall show later, it is not the certain insurance against riots that many people in Denver believe. Patterns of discrimination are less rigid in Denver, although prejudice certainly exists. Colorado has a model Fair Housing Law, though its implementation is not with-

out flaws. Governmental and private organizations interested in civil rights and equality of treatment are vigorous.
Moreover, the standard of life among minority groups in
Denver is higher than it is elsewhere in the country. For
example, the median income for Negro families in the
nation in 1966 was about $3,874.[2] In Denver the median
income was $5,000. In 1960 the national census put the
median income of Negro families in Denver at $4,642.
Although Negroes and the Spanish-named are concentrated
residentially in certain parts of the city, many characteristics
of ghetto living are absent in these areas. The association
between residential exclusion and depressed physical conditions is much less close in Denver than in many other
American cities.

At the time the study was made, Denver had a police
force of 813 men.[3] The ratio of policemen to population was
1.6 per thousand. This would put Denver toward the bottom
of the scale among cities of comparable size.[4] In fact, according to the FBI's recommendation for a minimum comple-
ment of policemen for a city of Denver's size, the city is
underpoliced. The FBI recommends a force of two policemen per every 1,000 of population. Thus Denver should
have a force of 1,100 men minimally.

The findings of the study are based primarily upon
four public opinion surveys. Each survey was directed at a
different segment of the Denver community. Let us examine
each in turn.

[2] *Sponsor,* July 1967.

[3] As of December 31, 1966 (Denver Police Department, *Annual
Report* [1966], p. 32).

[4] President's Commission on Law Enforcement and Criminal Justice,
The Challenge of Crime in a Free Society (Washington, D.C.: U.S. Government Printing Office, 1967), p. 96, gave the ratio of policemen per
thousand in cities of over 500,000 as being from 1.07 to 4.04.

Survey one was directed at the general public. The survey was based upon two modified area probability samples—one sample representing the majority population, the other the minority populations. Eight hundred and six respondents were interviewed: 336 Dominants, 234 Negroes, and 236 Spanish-named. Although the total general public sample was not representative of the population, due to the way in which the sample was drawn, each of its constituent parts was representative of a particular ethnic group. The extent of representativeness of the three subsamples can be seen in Table A. Generalizations about public behavior based upon survey one will be predicated upon major ethnic groups and not the population of the city of Denver as a whole.

TABLE A
COMPARISON OF SAMPLE (PHASE I) WITH 1960 CENSUS DATA

| | SAMPLE (PHASE I) | | | CENSUS 1960 | | |
	Anglo	Negro	Spanish	Anglo	Negro	Spanish
Sex: Male	42%	44%	37%	48%	49%	49%
Sex: Female	56%	56%	62%	52%	51%	51%
Median age	49.5	40	35.5	45	38	36.5
Over seventy	20%	6%	3%	12%	7%	5%
Median education	12	11.5	9.1	12.1	11.2	8.6
Median income (est.)	$5,333	$5,000	$4,333	$6,361	$4,642	$4,680

Interviews with minority persons were conducted generally by people from the same ethnic community. This was done in order to obtain the highest possible degree of interviewer-respondent rapport. Of the 470 minority interviews, only 70 were conducted by Dominants.

Survey two was an intensive study of Negroes and the Spanish-named. Subsamples were drawn from the highest-density Negro and Spanish-named census tracts in the city of Denver on a quasi-probability basis. Respondents in these subsamples were interviewed for periods of about three hours. In the intensive minority survey a hundred Negroes and a hundred Spanish-named persons were interviewed.

Survey three was of Denver policemen. With the co-operation of the Police Department and the Mayor's office, interviews were conducted with one hundred officers. Almost one out of every eight officers was interviewed. The sample was randomly selected from a roster provided by the Police Department. Interviews were conducted in the homes of the officers during off-duty hours. Interview schedules were not seen, received, or modified by anyone connected with the Denver Police Department any time during the course of this study.

The police sample was almost exactly representative of the ethnic composition of the force. Six percent of the force is from minority groups, compared with 5% in the survey. Within the minority portion of the police sample, Spanish-named officers were slightly overrepresented, while Negro officers were slightly underrepresented. Minority groups are not represented on the force in proportion to their numbers in the population. The Denver force is, as one can see, predominantly composed of Dominants. Comparisons between police officers and the general public will be made with the Dominant subsample of survey one. This is done because the Denver force is largely composed of Dominants and because the general public survey was not representative of the population as a whole but only of ethnic groups within it. The best comparison is, therefore, made between police officers and the Dominant public.

We might add that the cooperation of the officers interviewed was outstanding. Some of them were, of course, more reticent than others. By and large the interviews were frank and open, with officers becoming more involved and enthusiastic as the interview proceeded.

Survey four was directed at community leaders. Seventy-six persons were selected representing prominent politicians, governmental administrators, business and financial leaders, and members of the news media.

In accord with our thesis—that the nature of relations between police and citizens can best be understood by studying the constraints bearing upon both—the first four chapters of the book deal with formative factors in the behavior of the police and minority people. Chapter 1 examines the background of policemen, including important personality traits and the manner in which they are recruited. Chapter 2 deals with the images of police work held by officers and members of the public. The frequency as well as the nature of contacts between police and the public is treated in Chapter 3. Special attention is given to differential rates of contact with the police between Dominants and minority persons. Chapter 4 presents a description of the constraints upon police work which are a part of the occupation itself. The purpose of this chapter is to indicate what policemen are called upon to do in the community by the nature of their calling. In Chapter 5 we explore the perceptions and attitudes of minority people toward the police. We try to understand how they view the police and the importance of the police in their everyday world. Chapter 6 performs the same task for the police, showing the perspectives of policemen upon minority people and minority problems. Probably the most dramatic evidence of tension between policemen and minorities has come in the form of riots in America's urban areas in the past several years. Chapter

7, therefore, focuses upon violence specifically in an attempt to discover what kinds of persons look most favorably upon violence and what kinds of solutions to violence different segments of the community are willing to accept. The book concludes with Chapter 8, which underscores the lessons learned from the study about police-community relations. Specific points are presented which we believe must be taken into consideration in formulating programs designed to heal the breach between police and citizens—especially minority citizens—in contemporary America.

Acknowledgments

In the course of conducting a complex, extended research project many debts are contracted. Some people help directly, giving freely of their time and energies because they think work is important; others contribute indirectly, without knowledge of their importance, by helping to smooth over difficulties, by providing advice, by obtaining information, and in general by making life a bit easier for the people engaged in research. We should like to acknowledge a few of these debts.

Mayor Thomas G. Currigan and his staff enthusiastically received and endorsed the proposal for doing a study of this kind in the city of Denver. He and his staff promised the cooperation of the city and county of Denver and were as good as their word. We trust that this report will be a happy augury for productive cooperation between government and university at the local level. The study was made possible by a grant from the United States Office of Economic Opportunity, Washington, D.C. The opinions expressed herein are those of the authors and should not be construed as representing the opinions or policy of any agency of the United States government. We hope that our work repays in some measure the trust which their support of us implied. Harold Dill, retired Chief of the Denver Police Department, extended to us the facilities of his department. He made it possible to view personally various aspects of police work and allowed us without hindrance to contact members of the force for extensive interviews.

We owe an enormous debt to the patience, insight, dedication, and ability of Mrs. Wanda Miles—research assistant for the project—who was responsible for processing most of the survey data utilized in the study. We might add that she mediated between us and machines and absorbed most of the frustration involved in such a relationship. This was no small contribution. We are also indebted to Donald M. Cassata, who also served as a most able research assistant throughout this project.

We wish to acknowledge with thanks the contributions of the 2,079 citizens of the city of Denver who consented to be interviewed by our staff. They came from all walks of life, all manner of occupations, and from backgrounds as diverse as those of our country. By representing the entire community, they spoke in its name. We hope that our analysis does justice to their enthusiasm in participating and to their yearnings for a better community.

Finally, we would like to acknowledge the contributions of our wives and families. They gave in ways that can never properly be articulated and which can only be understood by grateful husbands and fathers.

To all these friends, co-workers, and agencies we extend our thanks, and hope that our work together will contribute to making this city—and this country—a more humane place in which to live.

D. H. B.

April 1968 H. M.

Contents

1

Who Are the Police?

Policemen are anonymous persons. Their uniform, badge, gun, and nightstick distract and hold the eye, obscuring the face and personal characteristics of an officer. In this respect policemen are like members of a minority group, to nongroup people they all look alike. However, behind the trappings of authority there does exist a human being. It is possible of course that putting on a uniform changes individuals in certain respects, making them more like all other policemen, but this does not change the basic fact that how a uniform is worn is determined in large measure by the nature of particular individuals. It is a commonplace observation that what people are socially, economically, racially, educationally, and religiously provides important clues as to how they will react and behave in their professional life. Consequently, it is imperative for people who would understand the actions of policemen in the community to study the men behind the uniform, and especially to find out who these men are in comparison to other members of the community. And it is even more important to determine the effects these individual human characteristics have upon occupational behavior.

Many people, treating the police as if they were all alike, expect too much or too little of them uniformly. Consider these two examples. Policemen are entrusted with substantial amounts of authority; they may interdict, arrest, and use force. This power frightens people and they therefore hope, possibly expect, that the men who wield this power are several cuts above the average. They imbue them, or want to imbue them, with qualities commensurate with their charge, in the same way that people want their doctors to be infallible, to be kind, and to lead an impeccable personal life. People want their policemen to be intelligent, sensitive, forbearing, insightful, as well as honest, reliable, and dedicated. On the other hand, precisely because policemen have authority and are generally seen by most people only in their authoritative roles, people sometimes assume that policemen enjoy being forceful and telling others what to do. They believe that policemen are authoritarian as a matter of personality, else they would not be policemen.

Our hopes and our fears, therefore, often encourage us to deal with the police undiscriminatingly and to fail to realize the individual human potential as well as shortcomings that may affect their behavior. Are they in fact capable of being better than their fellowmen, so as to bear responsibly the great charge set upon them? Or are they set apart from other members of the community in some fundamental way, so that they will be forever at odds with the community?

If we are ever to understand why police do as they do and to appreciate what they are capable of becoming, it is essential that we study who the police are.

THE BACKGROUND OF POLICEMEN

The typical Denver policeman is white, Protestant, has at least a high-school education, is married with two or three children, and has been raised in a community in the western or north-central part of the United States.[1]

Minority groups are decidedly underrepresented on the Denver police force. Denver's minority population—Negroes and Spanish-surnamed—is approximately 22% of the whole; in the police, minority members make up 5% of the force. This situation is not uncommon in American cities. Generally Negroes and Spanish-named people have not been attracted by police careers and until very recently have not been encouraged to seek them. In 1967 there were slightly more Negroes than Spanish-named officers on the force (23 against 18), although Spanish-named people comprise a larger proportion of the total population (12.9% against 9.5%).

The Irish, and especially the Catholic, policeman is not a fixture of the Denver police scene as he is of many cities in the eastern United States. Only 27% of Denver

[1] The qualifications for recruitment to the police are (1) citizen of the United States, by birth or naturalization; (2) ability to speak, read, and write English and possession of a high-school diploma or a general education certificate; (3) good moral character; (4) twenty-one to thirty-five years old; and (5) not less than 5 feet 8 inches tall and 145 pounds in weight. The candidate is asked to take a thorough physical examination, a polygraph test, and an oral interview. There are no residence requirements.

policemen are Roman Catholic, while 1% are Jewish and 41% Protestant. Among the Dominant public as a whole our survey showed that 23% were Catholic, 55% Protestant, and 5% Jewish.[2] Relative to the population at large, there is a slight overrepresentation of Catholics and underrepresentation of Jews.

The educational level of policemen is substantially higher than in the population as a whole. At the same time, there are fewer policemen proportionately who are college graduates. Forty-seven percent of the Denver population in 1960 had not finished high school compared to only 6% of the police who had not. Fifty-nine percent of the officers had finished high school, against 29% generally; 30% of them had some college training, against only 10% generally; but only 5% of them had actually finished college, against 10% generally. Since contact with the police is greatest among less well educated people, one can safely conclude that in the vast majority of instances policemen belong to a higher educational strata than the people they deal with.

Policemen are family men. In our sample of Denver policemen, not one was single. By contrast, among the adult Dominant population sampled, 70% were married. Moreover, policemen seem to have more stable marriages than are to be found in the community as a whole. Only 2% of the officers had been divorced against 5% generally. Policemen are also parents. A mere 3% of them had no children; two-thirds had two or three children and one-fifth had four or more. This is an important point to bear in mind. Policemen represent family men, men who value family

[2] The 1960 national census does not include data on religious affiliation. It was necessary, therefore, to rely on our survey to provide the required information.

stability highly and who may rely on their families for support against a populace which they often regard as hostile.

Denver and Colorado are well known for having a very high proportion of immigrants among their total populations. People frequently comment on how rare it is to meet someone who was born in the state, let alone someone born in Denver. Policemen, however, are predominantly local men. According to the 1960 census, only 13% of Colorado's population had lived in Colorado ten years or more. By contrast, 84% of Denver's policemen had lived in Denver for more than ten years and a full 40% had lived there all their lives. Denver policemen have seen the state and the city grow and change; they are not transplants from elsewhere, newly attracted to the area. While most policemen have not grown up in a large metropolitan area like Denver, very few grew up on a farm or in rural areas. Sixty-eight percent of them grew up either in a small or large city, as opposed to a town or a farm setting. Thus, while 40% grew up in Denver itself, another 28% grew up in places like Colorado Springs, Cheyenne, Laramie, Rapid City, and Grand Junction. Among the Dominant public in Denver, only 53% grew up in a small or a large city. Denver policemen have had a greater opportunity to become acquainted with "city" living than most people in the community, although "city" should not be interpreted as meaning the vast urban agglomerations of the eastern United States. This pattern appears to have been stable over time. No connection was found between the size of communities from which policemen have come and the age of policemen. Older policemen are as likely to have grown up in cities as new recruits.

The areas of the country from which the nonnative policemen have come are the same as for the community as a whole. The overwhelming majority, about three-quarters in both samples, have come from the West or the North Central states. About 8% are from the South and 6% from the Northeast. Denver's policemen, like its general population, are by and large not "far-trekkers," but have come from adjacent regions.

The social origins of Denver policemen are predominantly lower middle-class or upper lower-class. The occupation of the head of the majority of families in which policemen grew up was designated by the policemen as "laboring" or "skilled laboring" (39% and 17%, respectively). Another one-third said their father's occupation was in services or business. Only 6% came from professional families. Class origins may also be inferred from the education of their fathers. Thirty-nine percent had an eighth grade education or less. Eleven percent had some high school but never finished; 31% finished high school, about half of whom had some college education. These figures make an interesting comparison with the educational attainments of policemen themselves. Fifty-nine percent of all policemen finished high school and 35% had some college training. It is quite clear that policemen are upwardly mobile educationally and that their present occupation represents an advance over what their parents were able to obtain.[3]

It might reasonably be suggested that social origins may differ among policemen depending on the size of the com-

[3] This finding has been substantiated for policemen in other cities as well. See, for example, Arthur Niederhoffer, *Behind the Shield* (Garden City, N.Y.: Doubleday and Co., Inc., 1967), pp. 38-39 and John H. McNamara, "Uncertainties in Police Work: The Relevance of Police Recruits' Backgrounds and Training," in *The Police*, ed. David J. Bordua (New York: John Wiley and Sons, Inc., 1967), p. 193.

munity they come from. For example, there might be more parents who are college graduates represented among police-men from cities than among policemen from rural areas. This does not appear to be true. The only association that could be found between size of communities policemen came from their social origins had to do with occupation. There was a slightly greater representation of civil service, professional, and industrial occupations among large-city families than among families from small cities and rural areas. This is not surprising. One can conclude that al-though socialization experiences may differ in some quali-tative aspects between policemen from communities of different sizes, class differentials do not. Police recruitment will not obtain markedly different individuals, in terms of social origins, by selecting more from communities of one size than another.

A POLICEMAN'S SOCIAL POSITION

How does a policeman view his social status in the Denver community? What factors seem to contribute to his sense of social station? Moreover, is he relatively satisfied with his position and does he view himself as being able to improve the fortunes of himself and his family?

Class is the concept generally employed to indicate status of individuals within a community. It encompasses, basically, the marks of income, education, and occupation. Our Denver data show that in fact these factors are con-sistently associated.[4] That is, the higher any of these was, the greater was the likelihood that the others would be

---

[4] For the Dominant population, the chi-square values among these variables were significant at the 1% level. Religion, however, was not found to be associated with income, education, or occupation.

high as well. People with greater education are apt to have
higher salaries and more skilled, less menial jobs. People
in manual occupations have both lower incomes and less
education. Even more to the point, we found that among
policemen their use of class designations in describing themselves was consistently associated with their own educational
attainments, and that of their parents, and the occupations
of both mothers and fathers.[5] We can conclude, therefore,
that there is substantial agreement among people in the
community that class status is based upon income, education,
and occupation—for this is how they make these judgments
themselves—and that there is an association in fact among
these elements among the population at large.

Policemen believe they belong on the borderline between middle-class and working-class status, as opposed to
"poor-class" or "upper-class." Almost half described themselves as working-class and just over half said they were
middle-class. In comparison, 35% of the Dominant (nonminority) general public said they were working-class and
51% said they were middle-class. A greater proportion of
policemen than Dominant public, then, evaluated themselves more prejudicially in terms of class. On the other
hand, where 6% of the Dominant public thought they were
"poor-class" and 6% thought they were "upper-class," only
one policeman said he was "poor-class" and only one other
said he was upper-class. Like the majority population as a
whole, policemen tend to view themselves as being middle-
class but shade their assessement on the lower side of that
grouping. They seem to have profound doubts about
whether they belong fully to the ubiquitous and desirable
middle-class.

[5] Chi-square values were all significant at the 1% level.

Policemen enjoy higher than average incomes. At the time of the survey (1966), three-fourths of all Denver policemen interviewed earned between seven and nine thousand dollars.[6] While probationary policemen (there are only a few at any time) earn less than seven thousand dollars a year, 34% of the general majority population surveyed

TABLE 1–1

DISTRIBUTION OF INCOME AMONG POLICE, GENERAL PUBLIC, AND THE TOTAL POPULATION OF DENVER, CENSUS 1960

Annual Income	Police*	%	Dominant Public	%	Total Population of Denver	%
Under $1,000	0	0	10	3	3,658	3
$1,000-1,999	0	0	15	4	6,451	5
2,000-2,999	0	0	5	1	8,843	7
3,000-3,999	0	0	13	4	10,059	8
4,000-4,999	0	0	15	4	13,062	11
5,000-5,999	0	0	35	10	14,988	12
6,000-6,999	0	0	26	8	14,806	12
7,000-7,999	52	52	39	12	12,090	10
8,000-8,999	22	22	26	8	10,046	9
9,000-9,999	11	11	53	16	7,322	6
10,000-14,999	3	3	37	11	15,991	13
15,000 or over	0	0	25	7	4,946	4
Total	88	88†	298	88	122,262	100

* As of December 1967.   † Eleven percent failed to respond to this question.

earned less than that each year. Furthermore, according to the 1960 census, 58% of the Denver population earned less than seven thousand dollars a year. Denver policemen are, at the same time, underrepresented proportionally in the salary categories above nine thousand dollars. And no Denver officer at the time of the survey earned more than fifteen thousand dollars a year (Table 1-1).

[6] Fifty-two percent earned between $7,000 and $8,000 and 22% earned between $8,000 and $9,000.

TABLE 1—2

*SALARY SCHEDULE DENVER POLICE DEPARTMENT**

Position	Effective January 1, 1965 Annual Salary	Effective July 1, 1967 Annual Salary
4th Grade (Probationary)	$5,700	$6,000
3rd Grade Police Matron	6,384	7,020
2nd Grade	6,720	7,392
1st Grade Patrolmen and Policewomen	7,056	7,752
Detective Technician Dispatcher	7,728	8,520
Sergeant Custodian Radio Engineer	8,266	9,096
Lieutenant Secretary of Police Superintendent, Radio Engineers	8,870	9,756
Captain	9,542	10,500
Division Chief	11,088	12,192
Chief of Police	14,840	16,320

* From the *Annual Report* (1966), p. 4.

A new salary scale became effective for policemen in July of 1967. Although the raise was substantial in percentage terms (Table 1-2), it does not change the general finding that most officers earn between seven and nine thousand dollars a year. And the comparative conclusion still stands that policemen are better paid than the average Denver citizen.

The relation of policemen's education to that of the general public is very similar to that of policemen's income to the general public. Policemen are better educated than the average, but with fewer individuals represented among the upper strata. This is another way of saying that the police are more homogeneous with respect to education and income than the population at large, and that they are above average on both scores.

It is one thing to know where policemen belong in the status hierarchy of the community; it is another to know whether they are pleased with their status and whether it contributes to their sense of well-being as policemen. As a measure of their satisfaction with their position, policemen were asked how things had been with their families four or five years before and then if things had gotten easier, harder, or were about the same. Four out of five policemen thought things were either very good or pretty good five years before; only 13% said they were not so good. Thus policemen did not show a substantial amount of discontent with their general economic lot. Twenty percent said things had gotten more difficult in the past five years. On the other hand, 44% said things were easier and 30% that they were the same. Among the Dominant public, there was a greater amount of dissatisfaction: 29% thought life had become harder, while 69% said matters were either easier or the same. Our findings show, therefore, that police are not unusually dissatisfied with their lot compared with people in other occupations.

It is interesting to note that the proportion of policemen with working wives is three and a half times as great as among the general Dominant populace (44% vs. 13%). This indicates that policemen and their families feel impelled to supplement the policeman's earnings. Policemen feel that the economic lot of their families is by and large acceptable, but it is at the cost of their wives working. It seems fair to conclude either that there is substantial latent dissatisfaction with respect to salary scales or that the kind of people who are drawn into police work, by their nature and regardless of the rate of remuneration, feel compelled to work harder to obtain more. In short, while discontent with salary scales is not obvious among Denver policemen, there may exist deep within many officers a slow-burning grievance that they are not earning enough so that their wives will not feel required to work.

A policeman's expectations about the future are sanguine, very much more so than the Dominant general public. Asked if in five years they expected their families to have a harder time, an easier time, or about the same as now, three out of five policemen said things would be easier. Almost a third said things would be the same. And only 7% said things would be harder. Among the Dominant general public, three times as many respondents thought things would be worse, and only 28% said things would be easier. Denver policemen seem to look toward the future fairly optimistically. Furthermore, they seem to feel that what they are doing for their children will enable them to have a life which will be better than the policeman's own. Three-quarters of all policemen interviewed said they thought their children would have a better life than their own. Only 8% said worse, while 10% said it would be the same.

A Denver policeman's sense of well-being economically is unaffected by his age, religion, education, or social origins; no association was found between these variables and his sense of satisfaction. One cannot say, for example, that less satisfied policemen are older, or Catholic, or less well educated than others. The ethnic background of the officer may be an important variable here, but the sample of minority officers in the survey was too small to allow for a meaningful test. There is also no evidence that the rank of the officer, the area of Denver to which he is assigned, or his length of service on the force affects his satisfaction with his economic lot.

Considered according to objective criteria, Denver policemen on the average are better off with respect to income and education than the majority of the Denver population. Moreover, they do not exhibit marked dissatisfaction with their social lot, although they and their families seem to need or want more income, with the result that a large proportion of their wives work. The conditions of their livelihood seem to be somewhat at variance with their subjective evaluation of their social station. They are unsure whether they belong to the prestigious middle-class or the lower-ranking working-class. It would be reasonable to suppose that the social origins of the policemen might affect their perceptions of the class to which they now belong. For example, officers from more disadvantaged backgrounds might conceive of themselves in more pejorative class terms than those from more fortunate surroundings. Analysis does not bear out this hypothesis. Statistical analysis shows no association between social origins and officers' current assessment of their own class rank. Of course, if the labels "working-class" and "middle-class" have no emotional significance, then one could assume that, when almost as many policemen plumped for one as the other to describe themselves, it indicated only random choices. On the other hand, if these labels do have emotional weight—as we believe they do—then the responses indicate a profound sense of status ambiguity, quite apart from objective circumstances of income and education or of social origins.

Although a more complete analysis of this puzzle must be postponed until Chapter 2, there are two factors which might influence an officer's appraisal of his class status. First, he is likely to have a low view of his social position if he feels that the community as a whole looks down on him. One should find, therefore, that those officers who feel alienated from the community are more inclined to call themselves "working-class" than those who believe they are held in higher esteem. This proposition can be tested from the data at hand. Second, it may be that the nature of the work policemen do tarnishes in their own minds the status of their occupation and makes them uncomfortable in presenting themselves as middle-class. After all, police work is often physical, sometimes dirty, involves shift-work, and brings officers into contact with undesirable elements of society. This proposition, unfortunately, cannot be tested from the data at hand. It should nonetheless be borne in mind. Police officers in private conversation frequently note that unlike other "professional" people their work does not involve contact with their peers or better—as it does more frequently in the legal, medical, or educational professions —but with those individuals no one else in the community wants to deal with.

PERSONALITY AND POLITICAL PREDISPOSITIONS

In asking who become policemen, certainly one of the most intriguing questions is what kinds of personalities these men bring to police work. The difficulties of categorizing personality types are enormous. We have tried to use standard measurement tests which have been used extensively in the past, thus providing a basis for comparison. It must be admitted that the tests may be too crude and the personality shadings too subtle to produce meaningful results. We have specified the items making up the tests, and the reader must make up his own mind as to the importance of the results. The Denver police survey included items designed to measure anomie, authoritarianism, prejudice, and social distance.

The fundamental question is, are the personalities of policemen different in important ways from those of other people? On all personality scales the data show that policemen are absolutely average people, and when they do differ from the community norm it is in the direction of being better or more nobly disposed than their fellowmen. We find no evidence that particular personality types are recruited to police work. Let us look at the anomie and authoritarianism scales in detail; prejudice and social distance scales will be analyzed in Chapter 6, when the predispositions of policemen toward minority groups is examined.

"Anomie" is a term used to describe a state of mind in which the individual loses faith in the future and in his own ability to affect it for the better. An anomic person is one who despairs of improving his lot and can see little point in trying to do so.[7] Denver policemen consistently

[7] The questions used to construct the anomie scale were as follows: (1) In spite of what people say, the life of the average man is getting worse; (2) It's hardly fair to bring children into the world with the way things look for the future; (3) Nowadays a person has to live pretty much for today and let tomorrow take care of itself; (4) These days a person doesn't really know who he can count on; and (5) There is little use in complaining to the politicians because often they aren't really interested in the problems of the average man. In each case the respondent was asked to agree strongly, agree, neither agree nor disagree, disagree strongly.

scored lower on the anomie scale than the Dominant general public. (Table 1-3). Eighty-seven percent of the police respondents scored in the lowest two categories on the scale; among the Dominant public, 59% scored in these categories. In the next highest category were found the remaining 14% of the police officers and another 25% of the Dominant public. Thirteen percent of the Dominant public scored in the two highest anomie categories; there were no policemen in these. Police officers, therefore, are consistently more sanguine about the future and also have a greater sense of personal efficacy in shaping the future than does Denver's

TABLE 1—3
SCORES ON THE ANOMIE PERSONALITY SCALE FOR POLICE
AND THE DOMINANT GENERAL PUBLIC

Scores*	Police	%	Public Dominant	%
1-5	0	0	7	2
6-10	0	0	38	11
11-15	14	14	85	25
16-20	66	66	129	38
21-25	19	19	74	21
Total	99†	99	333	97‡

* The scores for the anomie scale can be interpreted as follows: the lower the score, the greater the anomie; the higher the score, the less anomie. Ideally, a score of 5 indicates the highest degree of anomie and 25, the lowest, if the respondent answered each question.
* One did not answer.   † One did not answer: six, or 2%, "don't know."

Dominant population as a whole. Policemen are less likely than the Dominant population generally to be fatalistic and despairing about life's possibilities. Their scores on the anomie scale support the conclusions earlier arrived at about the greater optimism shown by policemen about their family's economic future and their greater satisfaction with their present socioeconomic place in the community. The personality dimension of authoritarianism is subject to various interpretations. The measure that we have used was designed to show the extent to which an individual believes in the value of obedience, punitive sanctions, and strict adherence to moral codes.[8] Since the Denver public was not given the authoritarian questions in their survey, it is necessary to compare the officers' scores against those produced by other studies. The five-item authoritarianism scale used in our study was developed in 1950 for use in Springfield, Massachusetts. It was replicated in studies conducted later in Nashville, Tennessee, and Lansing, Michigan.[9] Comparing the Denver data with the latter two studies, we find that Denver police officers scored lower than the

[8] We have adopted the five-item F-scale developed by Leo Srole, "Social Integration and Certain Corollaries: An Exploratory Study," *American Sociological Review* (December 1956), 709-716. Srole found through latent structure analysis that the five-item scale met specifications for unidimensionality among the thirty items of the original F-scale. The thirty-item scale was heterogeneous in content. Srole concluded that the shorter version was a "purer" measure of authoritarianism and probably more reliable. The five-item F-scale is composed of the following statements: (1) The most important thing to teach children is absolute obedience to their parents; (2) Any good leader should be strict with people under him in order to gain their respect; (3) There are two kinds of people in the world: the weak and the strong; (4) No decent man can respect a woman who has had sex relations before marriage; and (5) Prison is too good for sex criminals; they should be publicly whipped or worse. Respondents were asked to strongly agree, agree, disagree, or strongly disagree.

[9] Edward L. McDill, "Anomie, Authoritarianism, Prejudice, and Socio-Economic Status: An Attempt at Clarification," *Social Forces* (March 1961), 239-245, and Alan H. Roberts and Milton Rokeach, "Anomie, Authoritarianism, and Prejudice: A Replication," *American Journal of Sociology* (January 1956), 355-358.

populations sampled in Nashville and Lansing.[10] The mean score in the Nashville survey was 14.3; for Denver officers it was 10.0.[11] In the Lansing study the mean score was 11.0; for Denver officers it was 8.57.[12] The evidence therefore suggests that Denver officers are less authoritarian than Dominant populations. We have no evidence to indicate that police officers are peculiarly authoritarian. Our evidence supports the proposition put forth by other observers of the police that people with authoritarian tendencies are not particularly evident in police departments.[13]

With respect to political predispositions, policemen tend to be more conservative and/or more Republican than the community as a whole. Political tendencies were determined in two ways in the survey: first, policemen were asked to identify themselves with respect to the political camp to which they felt they belonged—conservative Democrat/Republican, moderate Democrat/Republican, liberal Democrat/Republican; second, they were asked how they voted in specific recent elections. When policemen and the general public labeled themselves, there turned out to be as many self-styled Republicans as Democrats (see Table 1-4). One-fourth of all policemen were Republicans and one-fourth

[10] The samples are not strictly comparable. The Nashville sample was stratified by social class, although all classes were covered. The Lansing study was of white, non-Jewish, native-born Americans. It was a random sample and is very similar to the Denver police sample in social composition.

[11] Codes ran from 5 to 20.

[12] Codes ran from 5 to 15.

[13] See, for example, the comments of Niederhoffer, *op. cit.*, pp. 132-147, and McNamara, *op. cit.*, p. 194. McNamara administered the standard F-scale to police recruits in New York City and found that they scored lower than nonpolice people of the same class and in comparable occupations.

were Democrats; among the Dominant public one-third were Republicans and one-third were Democrats. Policemen were less willing than the Dominant public to state an affiliation, 46% of the policemen calling themselves "independents," against 32% of the public. Computing a breakdown of moderates and liberals together against conservatives,

TABLE 1—4
POLITICAL PREDISPOSITIONS OF THE POLICE
AND THE DOMINANT PUBLIC

Political Predispositions	Dominant Police	%	Public	%
Liberal Democrat	6	6	27	8
Liberal Republican	3	3	24	7
Moderate Democrat	11	11	63	19
Moderate Republican	11	11	43	13
Conservative Democrat	9	9	24	7
Conservative Republican	12	12	29	9
Independent	46	46	106	32
Other	1	1	0	0
Total	99*	99	316	95†

*For 1% the question did not apply.   † Five percent of the sample did not respond.

regardless of party, the data show a tendency for policemen to be self-styled conservatives more frequently than the majority general public. Of those officers who were willing to state a preference, 21% called themselves conservatives, against 16% who called themselves conservatives among the Dominant public. The data from recent elections is even more persuasive of the greater conservatism of policemen. In the 1964 presidential election, Denver as a whole went for Johnson two to one (see Table 1-5). The Dominant public, according to their own survey testimony, went for Johnson two to one. Among the police, however, Goldwater outpolled Johnson by two percentage points, 49% to 47%. As one would expect, there is a clear association between actual voting behavior and the political leanings revealed by respondents.[14] Republicans voted for Goldwater and Democrats for Johnson, although the more liberal the respondent, regardless of party, the more likely he was to have voted for Johnson. This relation did not show up in the gubernatorial or senate races in 1966. In those races

TABLE 1–5
REPORTED AND ACTUAL VOTING BEHAVIOR FOR PRESIDENT IN 1964 AMONG DOMINANT PUBLIC, AND TOTAL POPULATION OF DENVER

Actual Voting Behavior	Police	%	Dominant Public	%	Total Population of Denver	%
Johnson	47	47	165	49	143,480	56
Goldwater	49	49	79	24	73,279	28
Did not vote	3	3	75	22	39,472	15
Total	99	99*	319	95	256,231†	99

* One percent did not answer; 96% voted and 2% either did not vote or did not answer.
† 1,529 of the registered voters in Denver voted for candidates representing the following parties: Socialist Workers Party (1,045); Socialists Labor Party (103); and Prohibition Party (381). This information along with the distribution of votes for presidential candidates presented in the above table was obtained from the Denver Election Commission.

Democrats were far more willing to vote for incumbent Republicans—Love for Governor and Allott for Senator. This would indicate that Goldwater alienated many Republican voters. Since the police still voted slightly more frequently for Goldwater than Johnson, this is a strong indication of their conservatism. The greater preference of policemen for Republican candidates can be seen clearly in the 1966 Colorado senatorial and gubernatorial races. In

[14] The chi-square value was significant at the 1% level.

both of these the city of Denver gave a very slight edge to the Republican candidate, a matter of four or five percentage points. The Dominant public went for the Republicans not quite two to one. The police, however, voted for the Republicans three to one (see Tables 1-6A, 1-6B).

Something of the nature of the conservatism of policemen was revealed in answers to a general question about the

TABLE 1—6A
REPORTED AND ACTUAL VOTING BEHAVIOR
FOR ELECTION OF SENATOR OF COLORADO, 1966

Actual Voting Behavior	Police	%	Dominant Public	%	Total Population of Denver	%
Allott (Rep.)	73	73	136	40	87,763	34
Romer (Dem.)	23	23	80	24	81,035	31
Did not vote	4	4	102	30	88,800*	34
Total	100	100	318	94	257,598	99

* The number who did not vote is the difference resulting from subtracting the number of those who voted from the total number registered to vote; 162 of the total population who voted chose an independent write-in candidate, Walter Cranson.

TABLE 1—6B
REPORTED AND ACTUAL VOTING BEHAVIOR
FOR GOVERNOR OF COLORADO, ELECTION 1966

Actual Voting Behavior	Police	%	Dominant Public	%	Total Population of Denver	%
Knous (Dem.)	27	27	78	23	77,994	31
Love (Rep.)	68	68	145	43	94,707	36
Martinez (New Hispano Party)	0	0	3	1	3,461	1
Did not vote	4	4	100	30	81,598	32
Total	99*	99	326	97	257,760	100

* One percent answered "doesn't apply."

problem of the poor in urban areas. Officers were asked, assuming more money was needed to help the poor in Denver, which of several methods of raising it would the respondent most readily approve. Besides questioning the premise of the question and saying they did *not* think more money was needed, respondents could choose among the following methods of raising the funds: local Denver sales tax, local Denver income tax, local Denver property tax, and federal assistance from Washington. Forty-two percent of all officers sampled replied that they did not think more money was needed. Another 6% said that money now available should be administered better. Of the 49% who accepted the premise that more money was needed, only 24.5% said outright that they would favor federal provision of funds. Another 14.3% said they thought there should be a combination of federal and local initiative. Thus only about 19% of the entire sample favored any federal assistance at all. The bulk of the supporters of more money for the poor, 30% of the sample, thought that funds should be provided wholly locally. Denver policemen are not convinced that money is the answer to the problem of urban poverty, and those accepting that prescription tend not to want federal intervention. It is an interesting commentary on the possibilities for raising local taxes in Denver that no officers support a heavier levy on property; most of them—80% of those who were for local initiative in aiding the poor— thought funds should be raised by an income tax. The rest thought that recourse should be made to a sales tax or a sales tax and an income tax.

Analysis of the item on money for the poor shows that people who voted for Goldwater tended to be less convinced than Johnson supporters that more money was in fact needed.[15] Analyzing the 42% of the sample that did not think more money was needed, 45% of them voted for Johnson, 52.5% for Goldwater, and 5% did not vote. Thus Denver policemen were not only predominantly for Goldwater in 1964, but half of those who voted for Johnson doubted that more money was needed for the urban poor. This evidence reinforces the finding that Denver policemen are conservative in political philosophy regardless of the party with which they affiliate.

There can be little question that the proportion of Republicans and persons of a conservative political leaning among the police is greater than among the community as a whole and among the Dominant public as well.[16] But what is the significance of this fact? Apart from being descriptive, does this finding tell us anything about how police are likely to behave? Does it suggest what they will do when faced with various choices in professional conduct? The answer is that it does not.

For example, there is no evidence from our study that personality and political predispositions are associated. Among the personality dimensions of anomie, authoritarianism, and prejudice, none was found to be associated significantly with either actual voting behavior or self-

[15] The chi-square value was significant at the 1% level.

[16] Impressionistic evidence from two knowledgeable students of the police bears out this finding. Both Niederhoffer, *op. cit.*, p. 144, and Jerome J. Skolnick, *Justice Without Trial* (New York: John Wiley and Sons, Inc., 1966), pp. 60-61, mention the pro-Republican, pro-conservative bent among police. They studied, respectively, police in New York City and northern California. Niederhoffer goes farther and states that many policemen will be attracted by the John Birch Society.

labeling with respect to political tendencies.[17] There is no warrant in our data to argue from political predispositions of policemen to the nature of their personalities. It is particularly important to underscore that prejudice against minority groups is not concentrated more heavily in one or another political party. One is as unlikely to encounter a prejudiced officer voting Republican as voting Democrat.

Analysis also fails to show any correlation between political predispositions and an officer's occupational experiences or attitudes. Knowing something about an officer's political behavior gives no clues whatever as to what he expects from various segments of the city's population: whether he believes minority groups require stricter enforcement than others; whether he has been abused by a member of the public or sued; whether his morale is high or low; how he evaluates police treatment of minorities; whether he is for a civilian review board; whether he is frequently approached for informal discussions by members of the public; whether he sympathizes with the plight of the poor and minorities; and what is his appraisal of the propriety and utility of violent riots as well as nonviolent demonstrations.

Granting, then, that the political conservatism of the police is unrelated to personality or professional behavior, how does one expain the relatively greater amount of con-

[17] We did find that in the case of anomie there was a significant association with voting in the Presidential election of 1964. Policemen scoring low in anomie were more likely to vote for Johnson. Putting the matter the other way around: people less optimistic about the future and less confident of their ability to shape their destiny were more inclined to vote for Goldwater. This association was in an isolated case. In no other election was a personality dimension associated with voting behavior.

servatism among the police? An explanation commonly given is that political loyalties are a product of adolescent environment and current socioeconomic position. In the case of Denver policemen this does not, however, appear to be the case. Examining the data on how police voted for President in 1964, United States Senator in 1966, Governor in 1966, and on their own political affiliations, we do not find any significant linkage between these and the backgrounds of policemen. Their voting behavior and political preferences are independent of such factors as religion, race,[18] education, age, size of community in which they grew up, and the education and occupation of their parents. There was only one background variable that was significantly associated with voting behavior: in the 1964 presidential election policemen from the Mountain and Pacific Coast states tended to be for Johnson, while those from the north-central part of the country tended to be for Goldwater.[19] It would appear that the political behavior of policemen is not conditioned seriously by the nature of their backgrounds. This is particularly surprising in the case of religion. Among Denver's Dominant population there was a correlation between religion and voting: Catholics and Jews tended to contain a higher proportion of people who voted Democrat.[20] While, therefore, religious affiliation may weight political behavior among the public, it does not appear to do so among policemen. This would suggest that factors peculiar to the police occupation are operative in conditioning political behavior, and that these factors override prior determinants.

[18] The proportion of minority group people in the police sample is too small to be certain of this.

[19] The chi-square value was significant at the 1% level.

[20] The chi-square value was significant between the 1% and 2% levels.

From the Dominant-public data there is evidence that income differentials are associated significantly with political predispositions and with actual voting behavior.[21] Could it be then that police voting behavior and political predispositions reflect the tendencies of people of similar income? The answer is definitely no. In the income bracket $7,000 to $10,000 Denver's Dominant population, according to the survey, voted 85% for Johnson and 14.7% for Goldwater. The policemen, by contrast, voted 47% for Johnson and 49% for Goldwater. With respect to political self-identification, on the other hand, the police conform very well to the Dominant population with similar income. We have already seen that self-proclaimed Republicans and Democrats among the police are of equal strength; among the Dominant population they are very nearly at equal strength, 29.1% Republicans and 34.8% Democrats. Looking at the conservative versus moderate-liberal division among the police, there were two self-proclaimed conservatives for every three moderate-liberals, while among the general population there was one conservative for every two moderate-liberals. It would appear, therefore, that policemen generally identify themselves politically as do members of the population who have similar incomes, although there is a tendency for the former to be slightly more conservative. In the presidential election of 1964, however, policemen voted very differently from people in the population similarly placed economically. This suggests either that the election of 1964 was particularly sensitive in some way for policemen or that policemen

[21] The chi-square value for the association between political predispositions and voting for Governor and Senator in 1966 was always significant at better than the 1% level.

are consistently more Republican or conservative in voting behavior than people of like income. Although the former interpretation may very well be true in part, examination of the elections for Governor and Senator in 1966 show that policemen consistently support Republicans more strongly than other people of their income level.[22] We must conclude, therefore, that policemen by virtue of their occupational affiliation seem to be attracted by Republican and/or conservative political candidates. There seems to be something about being a policeman that either selects more conservative individuals or encourages them to become conservative after joining. Moreover, since the age of a policeman does not correlate with political tendencies, the conclusion that police work selects for conservative individuals would seem to be sustained, unless one assumes that the move to conservatism happens very shortly after joining.

That policemen seem to differ politically from people of similar socioeconomic status is borne out again by comparing the voting behavior of policemen with Dominants who have similar amounts of education. High-school graduates among Dominants who actually voted in 1964 voted 69% for Johnson, 31% for Goldwater; policemen with a high-school education voted 49% for Johnson and 51% for Goldwater. People with some college education voted 67.5%

---

[22] For example, the Dominant public voted for Governor 53.6% for Love, 24.1% for Knous; the police were 68% for Love, 27% for Knous. In the race for Senator, the Dominant public was 46.1% for Allott, 23% for Romer; the police were 73% for Allott and 34.6% for Romer. Even taking into account that there was a higher proportion of people who failed to vote among the public than the police, policemen still voted much more strongly for Republican candidates than Dominants with similar incomes.

for Johnson and 32.4% for Goldwater; policemen with some college education voted 51% for Johnson and 48% for Goldwater.

The propensity toward conservatism among Denver policemen is not a function of personality, still less is it a function of the economic and social groups which they have come from or now inhabit. It would appear that the prospect of being a policeman attracts persons of a more conservative bent or that being a policeman intensifies conservative propensities. There could be several reasons for this. The policeman is, by the nature of his calling, a defender of the status quo. His job is not to lead social revolutions or to militate for new laws. A person interested in vigorous social innovation would hardly adopt police work as a career. A policeman has a vested interest in maintaining uninterrupted and unimpeded the routine of community life, and he accomplishes this by enforcing existing laws. For this reason he is almost required to have what one author has called a "conservative personality."[23] By extension, what is unfamiliar and unconventional is disturbing to policemen—it requires them to reevaluate a whole series of judgments about what is permissible within the confines of existing law. Moreover, change and dislocation creates new demands upon policemen, either to enforce laws more vigorously or to disregard them more tolerantly. What is more, in recent years the issues of public order and safety, which are at the very heart of the police occupation, have been injected into partisan political debate. Certainly in 1964 these issues became identified with Goldwater and his brand of Republicanism. Furthermore, policemen may tend

[23] Skolnick, *op. cit.*, p. 61.

to be conservative because in a time of marked social insta-
bility, they, like many other individuals, instinctively yearn
for a time of greater calm—a time when events seemed more
manageable and understandable. The passage of time has a
wonderful way of making the complexities and uncertainties
of the present appear simple and relatively straightforward.
What is past thus appears attractive just because it is complete. Policemen, more than most people, have had to cope
in recent years with the violent, sometimes savage, manifesta-
tions of our changing social order. This may redouble their
fears for the future and their hankering for past patterns
of accommodation.

For all these reasons, therefore, men who select police
work as a lifetime occupation may tend to be on the conservative side of the political spectrum. And, equally plausible, people drawn into police work may find conservative
propensities intensified through constant exposure to the
demands of police life.

We must add that although policemen in Denver are
more conservative than the population generally or the
Dominant population in particular, it would be a profound
mistake to make too much of this fact and to conclude that
all police officers uniformly incline toward conservatism.
This is not the case at all. In 1964, when one presidential
candidate appealed very explicitly for order in society and
against "crime in the streets," almost half of Denver's officers
nonetheless voted for Johnson. Considering that in the 1966
electoral contests policemen voted almost two to one for
Republican candidates, Goldwater appears to have been
more than many policemen, even those with Republican
leanings, could take. Similarly, on the question of financial

assistance to the poor, more than half the sample thought that money was needed; they simply disagreed about where it should come from.

WHY DO MEN JOIN THE POLICE?

The study has shown that police work does not select for particular personality types. Denver policemen do, however, exhibit certain socioeconomic characteristics in common. They come from working-class or lower-middle-class homes; they have on the average slightly better than a high-school education; they were raised in the Rocky Mountains —Great Plains region; and they grew up in small cities or large towns and not in rural areas. Why do these men join the police? How did they manage to become involved in a police career?

Most Denver policemen tried some other occupation before entering police work. They did not move directly from school, whether high school or college, into police work. Although there is no official information readily accessible about the average age of recruitment to the force, it is possible to determine it from the survey data. The average age of policemen in our sample is about thirty-eight; the average number of years on the force is eleven. Thus it is safe to conclude that most of the men who join the Denver police are at least twenty-five years old at the time of recruitment. Most policemen indicated that they engaged in another line of work before joining the police; only 6% said they had not. About two-thirds of all policemen received some specialized education prior to joining the police. Thirty-three percent, for example, attended a special school while doing military service; 20% went to a trade school before joining the police. In fact only one-third of the sample said they had gone to no specialized school at all.

We can conclude from these facts that policemen were not determined at an early age upon the career they are now pursuing. Many of them may have first been exposed to police work in the military, but we have no information about that. Denver police appear to have accepted the police as a career after finding another occupation unsatisfactory. The reasons for their dissatisfaction undoubtedly were many and varied; the important fact is that police work was a second choice. It was a career whose merits had not been immediately perceived. Moreover, it is significant that about two out of five policemen worked first in a skilled trade or a laboring occupation. Another one-third say they worked in business or service careers. Considering that most policemen have only slightly better than a high-school education, it seems clear that they were not in executive or managerial positions. They were probably salesmen, truck drivers, laundrymen, grocery store clerks, waiters, repairmen, and so forth. Only 6% of them did professional work For men such as these a career in the police would hold out several attractions: security,[24] reasonably good pay, satisfactory promotion prospects, community recognition, and the prospect of varied, out-of-doors, and possibly exciting work.

In short, a career in the police would be a natural

[24] The city charter provides that a police officer may retire after twenty-five years service if he has reached the age of fifty. Upon retirement he receives a pension in the amount of one-half of the salary received during the year preceding the date of retirement. If an officer dies while in service, his widow receives a pension in the amount of one-third of the officer's salary. An additional allowance is made to the widow for dependent children under the age of eighteen years.

choice for young men, no longer adolescent, unsatisfied with other occupations, holding a high-school diploma, and coming from social backgrounds associated with manual labor, skilled trades, small entrepreneurial ventures, or modest positions in service occupations. Police work must have seemed a logical career alternative.[25] It is not an accident that individuals with a certain socioeconomic background are in police work; it is precisely such individuals to whom a police career would most likely appeal. One does not need a special theory to explain why men go into police work— as many police detractors would suggest. One explains recruitment to the police force as one explains recruitment to any occupation, namely, in terms of its status, rewards, minimal educational requirements, and conditions of service. There is no more reason to think that occupation selection for police work proceeds by a different logic than for careers as lawyers, doctors, automobile mechanics, radio technicians, and secretaries.

It is also possible that a career in the police force is not only a logical alternative for a certain class of young men but that it may exert an especially favorable appeal. Could it be, for example, that people with these educational attainments and socioeconomic backgrounds view the police in a more sanguine fashion than people placed differently in society? Could it be that within homes from which policemen come the police are regarded particularly favorably? We are in a position to test this possibility from the data at hand. The survey of the general public collected information on the importance people attached to the job of policeman, on the quality of the job being done by policemen in their neighborhood, and on the general reputation of the

[25] Niederhoffer, *op. cit.,* pp. 147-148, comes to the same conclusion.

police in the neighborhood. Analysis of these responses shows that views on these matters are not affected at all by differences in income or education of respondents. Evaluations of the police with respect to the importance of their work and the quality of job they are doing, in Denver at least, are independent of the most important indicators of socioeconomic status. Our data does not, therefore, support the proposition that the socioeconomic groups from which police are predominantly recruited are especially well disposed toward the police.

Recruits bring to police work the same kind of evaluations of the police made by people generally. They are neither more starry-eyed nor more cynical. They choose to be policemen because it fits their potentialities and promises the kinds of rewards considered by them commensurate with their background and training. By and large, it represents an advance over what their parents obtained. One understands police recruitment, then, in terms of a practical upward step in social mobility as well as an improvement in life prospects.

2

Images and
Self-Images

People regard policemen ambiguously. On the one hand, they expect them to offer assistance immediately and efficiently whenever the citizen requires. In the greatest of life's crises the police are appealed to automatically. It is true of course that most people think very little about the police, but when they do, they consider them indispensable and when they need them they need them unconditionally. Thus people expect a great deal of the police. On the other hand, police are often objects of great suspicion, if for no other reason than that they must "discipline those whom they serve"[1] and may use force in order to secure compliance. Policemen, then, are objects both of fear and awe; we expect them to be at the same time servants and masters.

---

[1] This apt phrase was coined by William A. Westley. "Violence and the Police," *American Journal of Sociology* (July 1953), p. 35.

The ambiguity at the heart of the police function suggests two points relevant to the study of the police. First, it is naive to think that people have a single attitude toward the police. Attitudes toward the police are dependent upon context. There is no point in posing as a single question what the community thinks about the police. The answer is it thinks many things. In order to understand police-community relations in any city one must study particular aspects of the relationship. One must always locate evaluations within a context of actions, needs, and expectations. Second, the police themselves are caught in treacherous crosscurrents of opinion that make their job more difficult. They must realize that the public views them inconsistently. Policemen cannot realistically expect to be held in high regard all the time, although they may hope that they will be respected some of the time.

A recurrent theme in this book will be an attempt to measure the expectations people have of the police in different contexts and to gauge the nature of their evaluations. For the moment, however, let us turn to the second concern and inquire about the general status-image of the police held by police and public alike and then determine whether they coincide. In this way we shall find out something about the psychological environment of the policeman. Does he feel accepted and respected in his profession or does he feel rejected and despised? Does he feel that because of his occupation he is a valued part of the community or does he feel that for this very reason he has been cut off from it? A comparative assessment of the public's general view of the police, oversimplified even though it must be, and the policeman's own self-image will provide an important insight into the compunctions and preoccupations that

policemen bring to their everyday contacts with citizens
of the community.

A POLICEMAN'S OCCUPATIONAL STATUS

A national-sample survey, designed to determine the
relative prestige of ninety occupations, found that police
work ranked fifty-fifth in 1947 and forty-seventh in 1963.[2]
While improvement in relative position was second only to
that of nuclear physicists, one still could not say that police
work was highly regarded as an occupation. In the Denver
survey, respondents were given an opportunity to indicate
the relative importance of the job of policemen. Being
important is not, of course, the same as being prestigious.
Among the majority community in Denver, 77% said the
policeman's job was either "much more important" or
"somewhat more important" than other jobs (see Table 2-1).
The minority communities were not as convinced, but the
discrepancy was not great. Seventy-one percent of Negroes
and 69% of Spanish-named people agreed that the job of
policemen was more important than other occupations.
Among the police, by contrast, 89% said it was more important than other jobs. And none of the policemen said it
was less important—as some of the general public had done.
It should be noted as well that policemen were much more
intensely convinced than the public of the importance of
their jobs: 61% said it was "much more important" than

[2] R. W. Hodge, P. M. Siegel, and P. H. Rossi, "Occupational
Prestige in the United States, 1925-63," *American Journal of Sociology,*
XXX (3) (1963), 291. Paul K. Hatt and C. C. North, "Prestige Ratings
of Occupations," in *Man, Work and Society,* ed. Sigmund Nosow and
William H. Form (New York: Basic Books, Inc., 1962), pp. 277-283.

TABLE 2—1

VIEWS AMONG DENVER POLICE AND MAJORITY AND MINORITY
GROUP MEMBERS CONCERNING THE IMPORTANCE OF THE
JOB OF POLICEMAN COMPARED TO OTHER JOBS

Importance of Job of Policeman	Police	%	Dominants	%	MINORITY GROUP			
					Negroes	%	Spanish	%
Much more important	61	61	146	43	80	34	91	39
Somewhat more important	28	28	115	34	87	37	70	30
About as important	10	10	65	19	58	25	53	23
Somewhat less important	0	0	3	1	6	3	4	2
Much less important	0	0	0	0	2	1	4	2
Total	99*	99	329	97†	233‡	100	222	96§

* One did not answer.   † One did not answer; six, or 2% "don't know."
‡ One did not answer; two "don't know."
§ Three, or 1%, did not answer; nine, or 4%, "don't know."

other jobs, while only 43% of the Dominants, 39% of the
Spanish-named people, and 34% of the Negroes agreed.
Thus, about half of the community as a whole who thought
the policeman's job was more important than others thought
it was only "somewhat more important."

The rating which members of the public gave the importance of police work was unaffected by occupation, education, or income of respondents.[3] This finding supports a
conclusion reached in Chapter 1, namely, that general
regard for police work is the same regardless of class.

Policemen do not believe that the public is as well
disposed toward their work as it really is. Asked how they
thought the public rated police work, 62% of the officers

[3] Actually, among the Spanish-named population chi-square analysis did show a significant relation between importance of the job and
occupation. The chi-square value was significant at better than the 1%
level. However, this was the only instance of an association of this
kind among the public.

said the public thought the job above average in importance. In fact, close to 75% of the entire community thought the job more important than others. However, where 61% of policemen thought the work "much more important," only 18% of policemen thought the public evaluated their work as highly. This is the first evidence for a proposition we shall examine more closely later, namely, that policemen tend consistently to believe the public regards them more harshly than it does in fact.

This study supports the proposition, frequently encountered in writings about the police, that there is a problem for policemen of "living with the discrepancy between the desired status and the perceived actual status."[4] Officers themselves see the police force and its personnel improving markedly in recent years. They believe that officers now being recruited are superior to the old, and they resent that the public persists in its old opinions when so much change for the better is apparent. For example, two-thirds of the officers believed that the manner of Denver police toward the public had changed recently. Seventy-five percent of these said the force was more courteous, more understanding of community problems, and more professional. Nine out of every ten officers said that a different kind of man was being recruited than heretofore—men who had more education, higher general qualifications, more training, and who were higher-caliber individuals.

In this connection it is interesting to note the characteristics that policemen want most to project. Although the answers to a question of this kind cannot be taken as indicating what policemen actually do or even think, it does indicate what they think the public most, or least, wants

[4] McNamara, *op. cit.*, p. 218.

them to be. Answers to this question provide a rough measure of what policemen think they must do to improve their public standing. In descending order of importance, policemen said they should project honesty, professional demeanor, equality of treatment, intelligence, good citizenship, trustworthiness, and tolerance. They should most avoid projecting being badly understood, deserving special commendation, being adventurous and glamorous, being underpaid, being pugnacious, deserving pity, being a "man's man," being just an ordinary guy with a job, being tough on offenders, being a "regular guy."

It seems inconsistent with a policman's self-image that he should be pitied. He wants to project a sense of being a professional, one who has integrity and stands for something greater than himself. For policemen, being a policeman is not just having a job; it means having a job which is crucial to the well-being of society.

RESPECT FOR THE POLICE

Of all the omnibus attitudes attributed to people concerning the police, respect is perhaps the most common. Moreover, it is the one policemen themselves consider the bell wether of public regard. Policemen want to be respected, and they measure their general status vis-à-vis the community in terms of respect. Although, as has been pointed out, any single attitude oversimplifies the wealth of evaluations made about the police, because of the seminality of "respect" in the minds of police and public alike it can be used to document the difference in general subjective judgments between community and police.

Policemen and members of the public were asked to compare the amount of respect for the police in Denver with that shown in other cities. The police had a rosier view than the public of the regard for them in Denver as compared with other cities (see Table 2-2). For example, not

TABLE 2—2

AMOUNT OF RESPECT FOR POLICE THAT EXISTS AMONG
THE DENVER PUBLIC COMPARED TO OTHER CITIES
AS PERCEIVED BY THE DENVER POLICE AND MAJORITY
AND MINORITY GROUP MEMBERS OF THE DENVER PUBLIC

| Amount of Respect | Police | % | Dominants | % | MINORITY GROUPS | | | |
					Negroes	%	Spanish	%
More	44	44	83	25	39	17	58	25
Less	0	0	35	10	22	9	27	12
About the same	36	36	193	57	165	70	121	52
Don't know	19	19	23	7	9	4	25	11
Total	99	99*	334	99†	235	100	231‡	100

*One did not respond.   † Two, or 1%, did not respond.
‡ Three, or 1%, did not respond; percent adds up to 100 due to rounding.

one policeman said there was less respect in Denver than elsewhere; among all sections of the public, about 10% said there was less respect in Denver. The judgments of Dominants and Spanish-named people coincided. Only the Negroes had a more jaundiced view: they were less willing to say that the police enjoyed greater respect in Denver than elsewhere and more willing to say it was just about the same as elsewhere. It would seem, therefore, that Denver policemen consider themselves fortunate to be serving in Denver; they believe the climate of opinion is better there.

The public was also asked whether they thought people were losing respect for law and authority. The vast majority did think so. Results were surprisingly alike among ethnic

groups, suggesting that people tend to read the general
trend similarly regardless of their own social position.
Among Dominants 75% agreed that respect for law and
authority was declining; among Negroes 80%; among Spanish-named people 69%.

A more informative finding was obtained from the
public in answer to a question asking them to evaluate the
general reputation of the police in their neighborhood. The
differences between the major ethnic components of the
community were marked (see Table 2-3). A majority of

TABLE 2—3
GENERAL REPUTATION OF POLICE IN RESPONDENT'S
NEIGHBORHOOD AMONG MAJORITY AND MINORITY
GROUP MEMBERS OF THE GENERAL PUBLIC

General Reputations	MAJORITY		MINORITY GROUPS			
	Dominants	%	Negroes	%	Spanish	%
High	180	54	52	22	73	31
Low	10	3	17	7	21	9
In between	81	24	131	56	99	42
Don't know	62	18	33	14	35	15
Total	333	99*	233	99†	227	97‡

* Three, or 1%, did not respond.   † Three, or 1%, did not respond.
‡ Six, or 3%, did not respond.

Dominants said that the reputation of the police in their
neighborhood was high, only 3% actually saying it was low.
The balance were "in between." Among Negroes, by contrast, less than one out of every four said the reputation of
the police was high in their neighborhood; among Spanish-
named people one out of three said it was high. From two
to three times as many minority-group members proportionately as Dominants said the reputation of the police
was low.

The low regard in which police are held in minority areas is palpably demonstrated in answers to a question about the type of job police do in a respondent's neighborhood. Less than half as many Negroes and Spanish-named people as Dominants said the police did an excellent job in their neighborhood, and more than twice as many thought they did a bad job. In this instance, the Spanish-named people were particularly dissatisfied (see Table 2-4).

TABLE 2—4

TYPE OF JOB POLICEMEN DO IN RESPONDENT'S
NEIGHBORHOOD AMONG MAJORITY AND MINORITY
GROUP MEMBERS OF THE GENERAL PUBLIC

Type of Job Done	MAJORITY		MINORITY GROUPS			
	Dominants	%	Negroes	%	Spanish	%
Excellent	91	27	29	12	25	11
Pretty good	196	58	167	71	152	65
Bad	7	2	16	7	30	13
Don't know	39	12	24	10	21	9
Total	333	99*	236	100	228	98†

* Three, or 1%, did not respond.   † Six, or 3%, did not respond.

Analyzing the foregoing general judgments made about the police, we find that ethnicity is correlative with certain judgments, but that class indicators, such as education, income, and occupation, are not. There is a suggestion that older people and women are more inclined to believe that respect for law is declining and for men to be more critical of police service than women. These associations are fragmentary, however, and do not show up for all ethnic groups.

Policemen tend to believe that public feeling toward them has generally improved in the past few years. At the same time, they are under no illusions about where in the community they are not held in high esteem. The vast majority of Denver policemen (78%) believe that opinion is now more favorable than it was a few years ago. Only 14% said opinion had moved in an unfavorable direction. It is clear that many policemen have as their baseline of evaluation the years of the Denver police scandal, 1961-62.[5] Many of them referred to that episode explicitly. The scandal was a traumatic experience for the department; police stock could hardly have been at a lower level than at that time. Thus when policemen indicate that opinion has changed for the better, they are really saying that the department has lived down those shocking years—which is probably a fair assessment.

It would be reasonable to expect that the views policemen have of the regard in which they are held might vary with their personal experience in the force. We have already seen that policemen consider regard for them higher in Denver than it may be for officers in other cities. This view is held uniformly by all members of the force, regardless of their rank, duty, location of assignment, or years on the force. Thus, even those patrolmen assigned to minority-

[5] The Denver police scandal attracted nationwide notoriety in the fall of 1961. Investigations showed that perhaps as many as fifty police officers had been systematically committing burglaries and thefts for private gain. There were also allegations of "payoffs" and receiving favors in money or kind. Not quite thirty officers were ultimately indicted and given jail sentences. The scandal did not involve any aspect of police-minority relations. Charges of "police brutality," for example, were not a part of the scandal. With a full investigation in 1962 of the International Association of Chiefs of Police and the appointment of a new Chief in 1963, after the municipal elections, the scandal could be pronounced closed. Although memories of it linger, the scandal is not an important fact for the study of police-minority relations in Denver.

group neighborhoods believe that they are held in higher regard than their counterparts in other cities. Among 78% of the policemen who believe public opinion has changed in their favor in the past few years, their personal experiences do seem to have played some role in their judgment. Analysis shows that location of assignment in Denver and the number of years spent on the force are differentially associated with whether they think opinion has improved.[6] Officers assigned to districts with minority populations, with large proportions of poor people, and which encompass parts of the core-city, tend not to view the shift of public opinion as much in their favor as officers assigned elsewhere.[7] The number of years an officer has spent on the force is also associated with his views about the nature of the shift in public opinion. However, the pattern is not easily interpreted. All that one can say confidently is that officers who have served only two or three years on the force are least impressed with a favorable change in public opinion. In fact, officers who have served on the force only two years are twice as likely to believe that the public has become less well disposed toward them than those who have served any other length of time. This finding may be important. Young officers certainly are not in a position to evaluate changes in public regard for the police on the basis of personal experience. But they may be experiencing what has been

[6] The chi-square values were significant between the 2% and 5% levels for location against perceived public respect; for years on the force against perceived public respect the value was significant at better than the 1% level.

[7] Officers assigned to District 1 are the least impressed by a favorable shift in public opinion; officers assigned to Districts 2 and 4 are the next least impressed; and officers assigned to District 3 and 6 are the most impressed. There is no District 5.

called "reality shock," that is, finding that their expectations about the life of a policeman do not entirely jibe with the reality of the job. Studies have shown that many professional people—doctors, teachers, social workers, lawyers—are apt to become disenchanted with their chosen occupation shortly after taking it up. They wonder if they have done the right thing. Most of them recover and, while not achieving quite the buoyancy they once enjoyed, they learn to live with and find satisfaction in the careers they have chosen. One can understand the substantially greater tendency of less experienced policemen to view a shift in public opinion as being unfavorable, especially since they have no personal basis for comparison, in terms of the theory of "reality shock." Before joining they thought police were well regarded. Now they find, on the basis of new and firsthand evidence, that police are viewed less favorably than they had expected. For them, in subjective terms, this may appear as a negative shift in public opinion.

Policemen immediately think of one of two groups in which there has been a noticeable decrease in respect for them in recent years—teen-agers and minority communities. Furthermore, asked if there were groups which had a particularly unfavorable view of the police—and 76% of the officers thought there were—officers once again singled out minority groups and teen-agers. Of those officers who did cite particular groups, 56% noted minorities. Teen-agers were cited by 14.5%, followed by criminals, at 9.2%. It is quite obvious that Denver police officers are sensitized to their relations with the minority communities. They have perceived—accurately, as our survey shows—that they are not as well regarded in minority neighborhoods. Interestingly, officers seem to feel that Spanish-named people are more unfavorably disposed toward them than Negroes. One-third of our sample that cited particular groups specified explicitly Spanish-named people. Only 5.3% mentioned Negroes explicitly.

Officers were asked to analyze the predispositions of youth generally to the police. Most of them thought there were important distinctions to be made among young people. With respect to the regard they show police, officers find children under twelve the most favorably disposed; teenagers not in college the least well disposed; and college students somewhere in between.

Looking at particular occupational groups and rating them in terms of their cooperativeness with the police, officers rated the following groups highest[8]—clergymen, schoolteachers, night watchmen, judges, business executives, storekeepers, and housewives. They judged least cooperative[9] —politicians, social workers, operators of taverns, intellectuals, writers and artists, lawyers, civil rights workers, and the unemployed.

It might be worth noting in passing that officers are not speaking off the tops of their heads; most of them have tangible evidence of the public's disregard for them. Ninety-eight percent of all officers report they have experienced verbal or physical abuse on the part of the public. Moreover, analysis shows that there is more than twice the likelihood that these incidents will occur in those areas having the highest concentration of minority and underprivileged people.[10] In sum, officers believe that minorities are not

[8] In descending order.   [9] In order of increasing noncooperation.
[10] The chi-square value was significant between the 2% and 5% levels. The Districts involved are 1 and 2.

likely to respect them, and they claim to have personal evidence for this.

Denver policemen seem to know that they are not universally respected and they seem to know the groups that like them least. At the same time, they may share a tendency to underplay the extent to which minority groups are critical of them. We have noted already that these policemen project more respect for themselves into the community, even among minority groups, than they think exists in other cities. And with this assessment the Denver public generally agrees. In talking about their general status in the eyes of minority groups, policemen frequently point with pride to the fact that minority group precincts always support raises in pay for the police when the issue is put to a vote. This is generally correct. In 1967, for example, when the latest pay raise was authorized in an election, Negro and Spanish-name precincts did cast a majority of votes in favor of it. They did not, however, support the police as much as policemen think they did. Comparing a selection of precincts representing the major ethnic and class divisions within the city, we found that the minority precincts had larger proportion of votes cast against the raise than is true elsewhere. In fact the only one of these precincts that turned the pay raise down was in a Negro area.

Policemen were asked in the survey to rate various groups with respect to whether they would support a police pay raise. Negroes were singled out by officers as being the group *most* favorably disposed. The next most favorably disposed group was said to be the middle-class. Officers thought the Spanish-named population would approve the issue, but barely. In fact, the most favorably disposed were upper-class Dominants; the least favorably disposed were Negroes, not necessarily lower-class Negroes. When the general public was asked in the survey how they would vote on the issue if they had a chance, Dominants approved it, Negroes strongly rejected it, and Spanish-named people rejected it—but not as strongly as Negroes.

The data, both electoral and survey, show then that minority groups will not go out of their way to victimize the police as to pay if given the chance in an election. The police, however, are fond possessors of a myth about the latent support they enjoy in minority communities, especially among Negroes. They have so gotten in the habit of using the electoral data as an indication that their stock is not dreadfully low among minority groups that they no longer appreciate the true thrust of opinion. While the police understand that police are a sensitive issue among minority groups, they seem to share a deep desire to minimize quite how extensive the disenchantment with them may be.

THE BURDEN OF BEING A POLICEMAN

Policemen in Denver are beset with self-doubt. They know they are not accorded the professional status they think they deserve. They want to be respected in what they do, yet they are too honest and realistic not to admit that certain groups in the community, especially minority groups, do not hold them in high esteem. They do not think that the situation is as desperate here as it has been revealed to be in other large cities of the country. And they want to believe that things are not as bad as many of their detractors, particularly civil-rights workers, would suggest. Policemen are aware, therefore, of their ambiguous standing. This is an appreciable psychological burden to carry about.

They have a deep feeling of being persistently and unfairly criticized. For example, three-fourths of all policemen believe that the complaints and criticisms directed against them are not justified at all. Fully 67% of those officers who said the police had been criticized by others in their presence stated that the person was mistaken and uninformed. Policemen think they know what troubles the public most: it is brutality and harassment, inaction, and traffic citations. Fifty-six percent of the sample named one of these pretexts. Officers think the charge of brutality and harassment is particularly unfair.[11] The survey asked officers what proportion of the charges of brutality and harassment they thought were true and well-founded. Nine out of ten officers said that not more than 5% were correct. The question for the present discussion is not whether their assessment is correct—we shall examine that in Chapter 5—but whether they believed they were being unjustifiably criticized. The answer is that they do.

Policemen are not particularly happy with the way in which they and their activities are handled by the public media—radio, television, newspapers, movies, and books. They thought the best job of informing the public correctly about the police was being done in Denver by television, followed by radio, and lastly the press. To illustrate, 58% of the officers thought that newspapers did a fair to bad job of informing the public about the police. Forty-nine percent rated radio as low, while only 26% rated television as low. In the opinion of policemen, the *Denver Post* does a better Job

---

[11] Two out of five officers cited charges of brutality or discrimination as having upset them most for being unfair.

than the *Rocky Mountain News*. Among the radio stations
there is not much to choose from, except that officers overwhelmingly consider KTLN to be doing a very bad job,
largely because of its alleged sensationalism. Three out of
five policemen also thought that movies, fiction, and television entertainment did not portray them correctly. Their
major criticism was that the picture presented was too simple
and unrealistic; it did not deal with the reality of police life.

Many commentators on the police have noted that
policemen are continually being made aware of being policemen. They cannot forget the role they play, and the result
is that they find it difficult to separate their public and
private lives. Our own study indicates this is true to an
extent among Denver policemen, but it is not as intense as
in other communities that have been studied. The vast
majority of officers (80%) recognize that an individual's behavior immediately changes when he discovers he is talking
to a policemen. Over half of all officers said that they find it
difficult to forget who they are; it is something they are not
allowed to forget. They don't, however, think their role cuts
them or their families off from normal social intercourse.
Only 12% said that it was awkward to make friends with
nonpolice families. At the same time, almost one-quarter of
the officers said that their families had complained of difficulties in social relations because they belonged to a police
family. An officer, then, is made aware once again that his
occupation does not instantaneously command respect but
actually may jeopardize normal social relations with people
in the community.

Their self-consciousness does not appear to have developed intense clannishness in their social relations. Only
18% said they associated mostly with police people; 68%

denied it, saying they associated mostly with nonpolice people. Officers do tend to live near other officers, although this may be due as much to economic reasons and an informal housing grapevine than to a strong desire to have support close at hand. A fourth of all officers said another officer lived in the same block or across the street. Fifty-one percent said the nearest officer lived within two blocks.

We found no evidence that those officers who felt most estranged from the public by virtue of their formal role developed clannishness in social life as a protection. It is possible that our questions were not sufficiently discriminating; it is also possible that respondents did not answer these questions truthfully. Nonetheless, we must say on the basis of our study that Denver policemen are (1) not as intensely clannish in their social life as other authors have stated to be true of other forces[12] and (2) have not adopted clannishness as a reaction to feeling cut off from the community by virtue of the role they play. Nor does analysis show that a particular type of policeman is more likely than others to feel estrangement and to be clannish. Finally, a sense of estrangement and clannish behavior is not associated with particular attitudes toward community problems. One might have thought that an officer's alienation from the community would be tied to an uncompromising, cynical, or unsympathetic attitude toward minority groups or a lack of awareness of his need for more training in human relations. There is no evidence for these suppositions. To the extent that officers feel alienated and tend to become clannish in social relations, these attitudes are not associated with general perspectives on police-community problems.

One important effect of policemen perceiving that they

[12] See, for example, Skolnick, *op. cit.,* pp. 52-53.

are held in low esteem would be upon their morale. Indeed, James Wilson has said, ". . . studies have shown that morale and job satisfaction are affected as much by the status of the occupation as by its internal management."[13] His own study of police sergeants in Chicago confirmed that finding. Another author has pointed out that the suicide rate among New York policemen is 50% higher than among the male population of the city as a whole.[14] He attributes this in part to isolation from the community and the resultant cynicism that permeates the force. Policemen in Denver report that morale in the department is high, and they testify that their own morale is even higher. To illustrate, 55% said morale in the department was "fairly high"; 25% that it was "very high." But 49% of them said their personal morale was "fairly high" and 43% that it was "very high." Analysis of the Denver data shows no association between morale and (1) the policeman's view of public respect for the police and (2) his evaluation of how important the public thinks police work is. We did find, however, that officers who are most self-conscious in their role tend to have lower personal morale than those who carry on with sangfroid. Thus, those officers who find that the behavior of the public changes toward them when they are identified as policemen have lower morale than officers who perceive no change in public behavior.[15] Even though a relationship between this survey's items on morale and respect, as well as occupation importance, did not show up, the fact of their status in the public eye is certainly very much on the minds of police officers. Asked what things they liked least about

[13] James Q. Wilson, "Police Moral, Reform, and Citizen Respect: The Chicago Case," in Bordua (ed.), *op. cit.*, p. 156.

[14] Niederhoffer, *op. cit.*, pp. 96-97.

[15] The chi-square value was significant at the 1% level.

being a police officer, the second most important item was
"public disrespect and understanding." The most important
item concerned occupational hazards, such as danger, tension, making arrests, and dealing with criminals. Twenty-one
percent of the sample cited these matters; 20% cited public
disrespect. At another point in the survey, a very similar
question was asked, producing almost identical results.
Asked to specify what was toughest about being a police
officer, 26% said job hazards, and 25% said public disrespect,
criticism, and misunderstanding. Officers were also asked to
state in their own words what kinds of things made for
high morale. Twenty-eight percent said good community
relations. Only "good working conditions" scored higher—
32% mentioned it.

As noted earlier,[16] officers did not appear to be sure to
which social class they belonged: almost as many said
"working-class" as said "middle-class." One explanation suggested for this sense of status ambiguity was that officers
who labeled themselves "working-class" may have been re-
acting to the negative regard they believed the public had
for them. One would find, therefore, that officers who labeled
themselves as being "working-class" would be more likely
than other officers to feel keenly the alienation between
police and public and to exhibit an awareness of distance.
This does not appear to be the case. Analysis shows no
association between class self-labeling and any of the variables dealing with a sense of estrangement from the public.
Thus it would appear that in Denver police officers' sense of
distance from the community is not deep enough to affect
their morale or to influence their perceptions of their occupation and social status in relation to those of others.

[16] See Chapter 1, p. 14.

THE POLICE AS A MINORITY GROUP

The relations between the police and community, and especially reactions of the police to their ambiguous status, are similar in several respects to those of minority groups.

First, policemen are very frequently thought of in terms of stereotypes. All of them are often described as being coarse, rough-spoken, rude, not very intelligent, and insensitive. Or they are portrayed as having similar personalities, especially in their addiction to authority and its trappings. Second, external features of policemen are often more salient than any others. People see predominantly the uniform; individual differences are obliterated. Third, they have a status in the community which is not congruent with their own self-image. They flinch from such denigrating comments as "Of course he's a cop, he couldn't do anything else" or "Does he work? No, he's a cop." Fourth, they are regularly treated to verbal and physical abuse. By virtue of what they are, they attract the hostility of the nonpolice community. They know what it is like to be apprehensive in contacts with their fellow men, not being sure if they will be received cordially or be subjected to tirades, invectives, and physical assault. Fifth, policemen are convinced they are systematically misunderstood. "Nobody knows the problems of a cop"; "if only we could get across to the community what a policeman's life is really like." These phrases echo repeatedly in conversations with policemen. Sixth, they are conscious of being portrayed persistently in the mass media in a simplistic, detracting fashion. They find themselves having become a stock character of fun or hostility. Seventh, policemen live in an environment of attitudes which appears quixotic and uncertain. They long to know the rules for winning approbation and seek them in vain. At one moment they are applauded for the important job they are doing; at another they are criticized intemperately for not doing enough, for doing too much, for being too tough, for being too lenient, for being too community-conscious, for not being community-conscious enough. Ninth, policemen are given formal authority but are frequently critized when they use it. Policemen are respected in principle but not in fact. Policemen are expected to know their place, whatever the pretense of formal status, and they should not be too eager, officious, pushy, or intrusive. Tenth, in search of support policemen turn inward toward their own colleagues and families for protection and approbation. They may find mixing with nonpolice people difficult; they may learn to avoid familiarity and in the end not even to search for it. In their professional life they instinctively protect one another, drawing together to support their own kind, fearing that people outside their own community cannot be relied upon to be fair and impartial.

To some extent most of these features of minority status apply to Denver policemen. To be sure, they do not all apply equally nor do they all apply as much in Denver as in some other communities. But they are present, and wear on the minds of policemen in Denver as they wear on the minds of other communities ambiguously situated in society. In short, there are several minority groups in America, and one of them is the police.

One reaction to their uncertain status has been to foster among policemen a pervasive, resigned cynicism. They simply can't allow themselves to believe they will ever be accepted in a more understanding, restrained, and sympathetic fashion. They have become inured to second-class citizenship. It is less trying emotionally to abandon hope than to risk committing oneself to change and then find one's hopes for greater acceptance dashed. Many policemen protect themselves by wrapping around them the cloak of cynicism. As they say to the inexperienced or idealistic officer faced with public inconsistency, "What else did you expect?" Such men as these will not be easily mobilized to new programs. Within police forces another reaction to their status situation—and a more constructive one—can also be seen. This is a movement toward what is called "professionalism." Basically it is an attempt on the part of policemen to rehabilitate their vocation by making police work efficient, self-critical, highly skilled, and by eliminating as much personal discretion in public contacts as possible. Although the rubric of "professionalism" covers very diverse programs, not all of them meritorious, the point to stress is that it is a creative reaction to the low status of police work in the eyes of the public. It is a program of self-improvement in the police minority-community.

Precisely because there is a discrepancy between image and self-image of policemen, police officers are vulnerable to change. Their own perceptions of their uncertain status are a powerful factor to mobilize for the improvement of police-community relations. It would be a profound mistake to conceive of policemen as being adamantly opposed to change in their relations with the community. In many ways, there is nothing they want more. This is not to say that they will accept uncritically whatever new programs are suggested. But critics of the police should realize that policemen themselves are almost pathetically amenable to rehabilitation. Those people who would renovate police-community relations would be well advised to build upon this desire for improvement that is a fundamental result of the policeman's minority status.

chapter 3

Contact

The basis for relations between the police and the community is created in actual contacts between members of each group. Contacts are not the sum total of relationships, however, nor are they the only determinants of predispositions on both sides. A single contact may set in motion an expanding circle of effects, conditioning the views of officers and citizens, views which they then carry into contacts with one another or discussions about one another. A bit of contact—especially of an unpleasant kind—goes a long way. If the student of police-community relations is going to be able to separate fact from fiction in the stories each side tells about the other, it is essential that he understand the nature of shared experiences between public and police.

By studying contacts between the police and the public one can also determine what the police are called upon to do. It will be especially important to compare what policemen are most attuned to accomplish in citizen contacts with what the public is most likely to demand of them. For this will indicate whether police and public hold similar opinions about what the police officer should be prepared to do in the line of duty.

Demands for service from the police are initiated in several ways. A task force for the President's Commission Law Enforcement and Criminal Justice specified four ways in which mobilization was initiated: first, people make calls for service by means of the telephone; second, people come in person to the station house; third, they contact policemen personally in the field and ask for assistance; fourth, policemen themselves perceive needs and respond on their own initiative. We shall now determine who contacts the police in these various ways, what the police are asked to do, what the police think they will be asked to do, and how willing different people are to ask the police for assistance.

PUBLIC CONTACT WITH THE POLICE

The survey shows that in Denver approximately four out of ten adults have had contact with the police at some time or other and that two and one-half out of every ten adults have had contact with them in the last year. Since the adult population of the city of Denver in 1966 was approximately 329,000,[1] the police department has had contact in the line of duty during the previous year with about 75,000 people. These were not trivial contacts, as would be the case

[1] The population in December 1966 was estimated by the Denver Planning Commission as being 521,896. According to the 1960 census, 36.8% of the population in Denver was twenty years of age or under. The figure for the adult population of Denver in 1966 was calculated by using the 1960 proportion of adults to nonadults.

in asking an officer for directions or for the correct time.
The survey asked people to enumerate contacts in which
(1) they made a request for help when something happened
which they felt required police attention (they were given
the example of something having been stolen from them) or
(2) they, or some member of their immediate family, had
"difficulties or troubles" they talked over with the police.
The survey made a deliberate effort to record only those
contacts which would be perceived by the public to be
important and where, as a result, the treatment received
from the police would be deemed important. We can conclude, therefore, that the police department has had what
might be called sensitive contact with almost 40% of the
adult population at sometime or other and with about 25%
of the adult population within the last year.[2]

The total amount of sensitive contact with the police
varied slightly according to ethnic group involved (see
Table 3-1). Contrary to popular impression, contact was
higher proportionately among the Dominant community
than among Negroes and Spanish-named. Ethnicity did not
affect the proportion of people that called the police for
help. Negroes called for assistance in as large proportions as

[2] This conclusion assumes that the survey year, 1966, was not
atypical. We have no reason to believe that it was. We might also
note that memories of calling the police for help fade fairly rapidly
or are blotted out by new contacts. In our study we found that of
the people who made a call for help, half of them made the call in
the preceding year. It is hard to believe that there were as many calls
upon the police in the past year as in all the previous years taken
together. Our data confirms, therefore, the finding of *Studies in Crime
and Law Enforcement in Major Metropolitan Areas,* Vol. I (Washington, D.C.: U.S. Government Printing Office, 1967), p. 37. This was a
report of a field survey prepared for the President's Commission on
Law Enforcement and Criminal Justice.

Dominants. At the same time, minority people are much less likely than Dominants to have talked over a problem with the police. Among Denver's two minority communities, Spanish-named people are less likely to have done so than Negroes. Arrest figures show that a larger proportion of minority group members are in trouble with the police than

TABLE 3—1

CALLS FOR ASSISTANCE FROM THE POLICE
WITHIN THE PAST YEAR BY DIFFERENT ETHNIC GROUPS

| | MAJORITY | | MINORITY GROUPS | | | |
	Dominants	%	Negroes	%	Spanish	%
Less than 6 months ago	45	13	32	14	34	15
6 months to 1 year ago	35	10	20	8	21	9
Total	80	23	52	22	55	24

Have Discussed a Problem With the Police Within the Past Year

	44	13	13	6	8	3

are members of the majority community.[3] It is significant, therefore, that though minority people might have more difficulties they might discuss with the police, fewer of them proportionately have actually done so. Dominants certainly have greater faith in the usefulness of talking things over with policemen than do members of minority groups.

There is other evidence for this contention as well. Our survey shows that when it comes to discussing problems with

[3] *The Challenge of Crime in a Free Society,* p. 44, noted that Negroes have a significantly higher rate of arrest in every offense category except certain offenses against public order and morals. The Denver Police Department does not keep records of the ethnicity of offenders. One assumes that the national pattern noted by the President's Commission holds true in Denver.

state and municipal agencies, the police play a larger role in the world of the Dominant citizen than in the worlds of the Negro or Spanish-named citizen. This is especially important when one recognizes, first, that the involvement of minorities with law-enforcement agencies is proportionately greater than among Dominants and, second, that minority people have more problems they discuss with municipal and state agencies generally than do Dominants (see Table 3-2). Twenty-five percent of Dominant respondents said they, or a member of their immediate family, had discussed some

TABLE 3–2

WHETHER OR NOT RESPONDENT OR MEMBERS OF HIS FAMILY HAD ANY DIFFICULTIES HE DISCUSSED WITH DEPARTMENTS OR AGENCIES IN THE PAST YEAR AMONG MAJORITY AND MINORITY GROUP MEMBERS OF THE GENERAL PUBLIC

| | MAJORITY | | MINORITY GROUPS | | | |
	Dominants	%	Negroes	%	Spanish	%
Yes	85	25	78	33	88	38
No	240	71	152	64	139	59
Total	325	96*	230	97†	227	97§

* Eleven, or 3%, did not respond.   † Six, or 3%, did not respond.
‡ Six, or 3%, did not respond.

trouble or difficulty with a state or municipal agency during the past year; among minorities, 33% of the Negroes and 38% of the Spanish-named had done the same. Yet among those people who had contacted agencies, a much greater proportion of Dominants had dealt with police than was the case among either Negroes or Spanish-named. Thirteen percent of all Dominants had discussed some difficulty with the police, but only 6% of Negroes and 3% of Spanish-named had done so. The state and municipal agencies that were contacted most frequently were for Dominants—in descending order—police department, sanitation department, public works department, Denver Welfare Department, municipal and juvenile courts. Among Negroes the most frequently contacted agencies were Colorado State Employment Service, Neighborhood Health Center, Denver Welfare Department, and Denver General Hospital. Among Spanish-named people the most important agencies were Denver Welfare Department, Neighborhood Health Center, Denver General Hospital, along with the Colorado State Employment Service and Juvenile Courts, and Denver Housing Authority with the War on Poverty.

The importance of these different agencies in the life of different ethnic communities is certainly eloquent testimony to the problems of minority groups in modern American society and to the relative standing of the police within these communities, especially when one assumes, plausibly in our view, that occasions for contact with the police are greater for minority group individuals.

Reasons for calling the police varied somewhat among ethnic groups. For all groups, thefts were the most common complaint, accounting for 33% to 41% of all calls for assistance (see Table 3-3). The second most important reason among Dominants for requesting help was auto accidents; among Negroes it was sickness; and among Spanish-named people complaints about a neighbor. Auto accidents were the third most important reason for Negro calls, but were not among the top seven reasons for the Spanish-named. Like Negroes, Spanish-named people called upon the police for help in times of sickness, this reason being the third most important for them. Two conclusions may be drawn from these facts. First, to some extent the nature of calls for

TABLE 3—3

REASONS RESPONDENTS NEEDED HELP FROM THE POLICE

| | MAJORITY DOMINANTS | | | MINORITY GROUPS | | | | | |
| | | | | NEGROES | | | SPANISH | | |
	Nos.	% of those who re-quested help	% of Dominant sample	Nos.	% of those who re-quested help	% of Negro sample	Nos.	% of those who re-quested help	% of Spanish sample
Theft	61	34.2	18	43	41.6	18	32	33.3	14
Gunfire	5	2.8	1	3	2.9	1	0	0.0	0
Auto accidents	25	14.0	7	10	9.7	4	6	6.1	3
Neighbor complaint	17	9.6	5	7	6.8	3	15	15.2	6
Vandalism	16	9.0	5	4	3.9	2	8	8.1	3
Prowler	16	9.0	5	4	3.9	2	6	6.1	3
Sickness	6	3.4	2	1	10.7	0	8	8.1	3
Animal problems	6	3.4	2	5	4.8	2	2	2.1	1
Personal attack	13	7.3	4	8	7.8	3	7	7.1	3
Lost person	5	2.8	1	2	1.9	1	7	7.1	3
Family problem	4	2.2	1	3	2.9	1	7	7.1	3
Protection	2	1.1	1	2	2	1	1	0.0	0
Other	2	1.1	1	1	1	0	0	0.0	0
Total	178*		53%	103†		38%	99‡		42%

* For 150 respondents, or 45% of the sample, the questions did not apply; 8 respondents, or 2% of the sample, did not respond.

† For 129 respondents, or 55% of the sample, the question did not apply; 2 respondents, or 1% of the sample, could not recall; and 2 respondents, or 1% of the sample, did not respond.

‡ For 130 respondents, or 56% of the sample, the question did not apply; 5 respondents, or 2% of the sample, did not respond.

police assistance depends upon social class, especially income. In the case of Negroes and Dominants, an association was found between income and reasons for calling the police.[4] Second, people with low incomes call upon the police in noncriminal personal emergency situations much more than people with higher incomes. As a result, one finds that Negroes and Spanish-named people call for police help in times of illness much more than do Dominants—in fact from two to three times more often. This finding supports what

[4] The chi-square value was significant at the 1% level.

police officers commonly say, that they are often called into low-income homes, very frequently minority-group homes, in order to determine whether someone needs to be hospitalized. If the officer does decide medical attention is required, he will be the one who will call for the ambulance from the municipal hospital.

We do not find any evidence that the sheer volume of calls made to the police for help or discussions with police about problems varies with economic position.[5] We find that contact per se with the police is unaffected by age, occupation, education, religion, income, or sex of the respondent. It might be noted in passing that within the Dominant community women are much more likely to have discussed a problem with the police than are men.[6] Women are not as likely, however, to have called the police for assistance.

One intriguing question is whether contact influences evaluations people make about the police. Can one say, for example, that any contact is likely to bias attitudes one way or the other? Or are particular evaluations of the police associated with having made demands upon the police for service? These questions must be distinguished from asking about the effects upon attitudes of unpleasant experiences. This latter topic will be taken up in Chapter 5. For the moment, we are concerned only with whether having made contact with the police affects evaluations of them. Analysis shows that people who have discussed a problem with the police—as distinct from calling them for help—are more apt than others to evaluate the service the police provide un-

[5] Sometimes within ethnic groups one factor, such as age or sex, may be related to contact, but this is never true for all groups—or even for any two—within Denver.

[6] They were three times as likely to have done so. The chi-square value was significant at better than the 1% level.

favorably. For example, among Dominants with police experience, 5% thought the police provided better service to their neighborhood than elsewhere and 8% thought the service was worse. Among Dominants *without* police experience, however, 15% thought the service was better in their neighborhood than elsewhere and less than 1% thought it worse. Among Negroes who had a discussion with the police about a problem, opinions about the police tended to be polarized. That is, people who had experience with the police were more likely to be both more critical and more laudatory about the quality of the job police did in their neighborhood. In effect, after experience with the police, Negroes had more pronounced opinions, both favorable and unfavorable. Polarization also took place among Negroes on the question of the reputation the police had in the neighborhood. More of those with experience thought it was both higher and lower than those who had no experience. People without experience, therefore, had not made up their minds; they were more inclined to give an indeterminate assessment.

Having called the police for help is associated with different attitudes depending upon the ethnic group involved. There are no correlations whatever for Dominants between having called upon the police for help and any evaluative attitude toward the police. The attitudes of Dominants toward the police are unaffected by having made a demand for service. For Negroes, by contrast, contact in a demand situation tends to be associated with more favorable evaluations of police function than among people without such experience. To illustrate, 35% of the Negroes who had made a demand upon the police thought that police reputation in their neighborhood was high; 10% of them thought it was low. Among Negroes without this experience, only 19%

thought the reputation of the police was high and 7.5% said it was low. Having called upon the police for help was also associated, among Negroes, with a more favorable evaluation of the service received from the police in their neighborhood compared with elsewhere and with a more favorable view of the treatment minorities receive at the hands of the police. Since the data do not allow us to determine the direction of cause-effect, if any, we could say with equal plausibility that people who are inclined to believe that police treat minorities fairly and will give satisfactory service in the immediate neighborhood are more likely to call upon the police for help than people who do not share these views. One bit of evidence suggests that attitudes may be more affected by contact than rate of contact by attitudes. There is a correlation for Negroes between making a demand and evaluations of the job the police do in the neighborhood. However, the evaluations associated with contact are polarized ones. That is, contact is higher among people both who think police service is excellent and those who think it is bad. It seems unlikely that if attitudes affected willingness to contact, people of positive and negative views would both show higher rates of contact. It is more reasonable to conclude that, although attitudes may affect willingness to contact in some measure, particularly at the extremes, contact with the police has the greater effect on attitudes—producing, in this case, firmer opinions, both favorable and unfavorable.

The linkage between having made a demand on the police and evaluations of them is less straightforward in the case of Spanish-named persons. Spanish-named people who have made a call for police assistance are more inclined than others to think the service the police give their neighborhoods is less good than elsewhere. This point is important because it indicates that, for Spanish-named persons at least, the direction of effect between contact and evaluations runs from contact to attitude-formation. It is hard to believe that persons with less favorable views of police service would be more inclined to call the police than others. It is not unreasonable to conclude that people with more contact have less favorable attitudes. Analysis also shows that for Spanish-named persons those with contact are also more likely to view favorably the treatment minorities receive at the hands of the police. Once again, one might argue that people with the more favorable dispositions are more likely to have called for help than others.

Generally, then, contact with the police—ignoring for the moment its character—is associated with several evaluations people make about the police. The association is slight for Dominants; it is also unfavorable to the police. For Negroes the association is greater, that is, touching more evaluations, and the relation is favorable to the police or, at worst, polarizes opinion. The linkage is stronger for Spanish-named persons than for Dominants, though weaker than among Negroes. The nature of the relation in the case of Spanish-named persons is indeterminate. It is not clear whether contact and favorable evaluations are associated or contact and unfavorable evaluations. There is some of both.

On the basis of this analysis, we suggest two tentative conclusions. First, it appears to us that contact is more important for the evaluations a person holds than the evaluations a person holds are for his willingness to contact the police, although we are not denying that particularly unfavorable views of the police may discourage a person from calling for police assistance. Second, the extent to which contact affects attitudes is a product, at least in part, of the sensitivity of the respondent's relations with the police. Thus, for Dominants there is by and large very slight association between contact and evaluations. If the direction of cause and effect is as we have stipulated, one concludes that for Dominants contact is uninformative; it does not cause them to reevaluate the police, because they are not particularly sensitized to the relationship. For Negroes, however, contact with the police is very informative, for one finds contact linked with several kinds of evaluations. Negroes do not enter into nor walk away from contact with the police indifferently. On the contrary, it is terribly significant for them, and they learn from it. It does affect their perceptual world. The Spanish-named occupy an intermediate position—more affected than Dominants, less affected than Negroes.

If one grants that contact does affect attitudes, then it follows that, with Negroes at least, the Denver police appear in a relatively favorable light. For to the extent that contact does affect evaluations, it affects Negro attitudes favorably for the most part; at worst, it polarizes them, and is as likely to make friends as enemies. There is certainly no evidence that contact with the police invariably disposes people to view the police more harshly. This is not the case, regardless of the ethnic group one considers.

POLICEMEN AS PEACE OFFICERS

One of the most common misconceptions about police work is that officers are primarily engaged in enforcing the law. Peculiarly, and perhaps damagingly, policemen themselves seem to share this view. While it would be fair to say that the primary duty formally placed upon them is to enforce the law, it would be wrong to conclude that this is what they spend most of their time doing. Police contact with the public is not primarily punitive, ending in giving a citation for an offense or in making an arrest. For example, about two-thirds of all officers interviewed in Denver said that not more than 9% of their contacts with the public resulted in a citation or an arrest.[7] Policemen, especially patrolmen, spend most of their time interceding and rendering assistance in nonpunitive ways. They interrupt behavior many more times than they punish it. For example, they tell crowds to move on, warn a man soliciting a prostitute to go somewhere else, admonish a drunk to behave and perhaps put him in a taxi and send him home. They interrupt activity on lovers' lanes, prevent a fist-fight from breaking out, or intervene between husbands and wives whose tempers have gotten the better of them. To be sure, the threat of punishment is always present, but it is employed much more rarely—proportionate to the number of contacts—than most people realize. As the President's Commission on Law Enforcement and Criminal Justice has said: ". . . it is apparent that he [the police officer] spends considerably more time keeping order, settling disputes, finding missing children, and helping drunks than he does in responding to criminal conduct which is serious enough to call for arrest, prosecution, and conviction"[8] For this reason many careful observers of the police believe it would be

[7] Niederhoffer, *op. cit.*, p. 26, in a footnote cites a study carried out by the Research Division of the International Association of Chiefs of Police in Syracuse, New York, in which it was found that the proportion of enforcement calls in police work amounted to not more than 20% and perhaps less than 10% of all calls.

[8] The President's Commission on Law Enforcement and Criminal

more accurate to describe policemen, especially patrolmen, as "peace officers" rather than "law officers."[9]

But there is more to the misconception about what police do than simply the mistaken notion that their contacts with the public are predominantly punitive. One of the major problems for policemen is to decide when the law should be enforced. Many nonpolice people, and some officers, talk as if the primary problem for policemen was the actual making of arrests. Punitive actions are certainly awkward and sometimes dangerous, but what is often obscured is the fact that situations are not open and shut with respect to whether the law has been sufficiently violated to warrant punishment. The law is not self-enforcing, and because its strictures rarely coincide exactly with real human situations or with the temper of the community at a given moment about the seriousness of an offense, judgment is required in its application. Not only, therefore, do most police contacts not involve even the opportunity to apply punitive sanctions but many contacts are ambiguous with respect to whether the criminal law should be applied. Policemen, though they frequently deny it in public, possess enormous discretion. They are not automata mechanically engaged in arresting people whenever certain lines are overstepped. Contact with the public is a decision-making action, except in that very small minority of cases in which the offense is so serious and so obvious that duty is clear.

In making a decision to arrest or to cite for an offense,

Justice, *Task Force Report: The Police* (Washington, D.C.: U.S. Government Printing Office, 1967), p. 13.

[9] Michael Banton, *The Policeman in the Community* (New York: Basic Books, Inc., 1964).

many considerations, quite extraneous to the strict canons of law, come into play. Public morality is one factor, and policemen share this morality. For example, people think it is wrong for a wife and children to pay twice for a husband's drunkenness; it is bad enough, many people reason, that the husband has squandered their meager livelihood and perhaps abused them, why compound the harm by arresting him and depriving them of all support? The public thinks that on certain holidays, especially New Year's and Christmas Eve, people should be given a little extra leeway. At the same time, it is also considered right and proper that roughnecks and bullies should be treated more severely than others.[10] Knowing the difficulties of obtaining convictions, policemen hesitate to arrest unless they know the evidence is sufficient to make a case. Or they may not arrest because they know the result isn't worth the effort, that the individual will be out of jail very soon or that the lesson of arrest will be ineffective.[11] This is often true in prostitution and drug addiction cases. Moreover, officers often internalize a scale of seriousness about offenses that effects when they make an arrest. They do not arrest every person who fails to stop completely at a stop sign, but they may do so at a school intersection. For a host of reasons, then, police contacts wtih the public involve the making of critical and very difficult decisions. A policeman is a "peace officer" not only because the application of legal sanctions in many instances is not an issue but because he is unavoidably faced with deciding if it is appropriate at all.

[10] For a short discussion of this point, see Banton, p. 146.

[11] See, for example, James Mills, "The Detective," *Life,* December 3, 1965, p. 90.

This fact should be recognized by police and public alike. As the President's Commission on Law Enforcement and Criminal Justice has said:

> . . . the police should openly acknowledge that, quite properly, they do not arrest all, or even most, offenders they know of. Among the factors accounting for this exercise of discretion are the volume of offenses and the limited resources of the police, the ambiguity of and the public desire for nonenforcement of many statutes and ordinances, the reluctance of many victims to complain and, most important, an entirely proper conviction by policemen that the invocation of criminal sanctions is too drastic a response to many offenses.[12]

In short, the nature of police contact with the public is a good deal more complex than is generally understood.

Policemen themselves, our survey shows, have definite ideas about the situations which pose particularly difficult problems for them as to whether to apply the sanctions of the law or not. Thirty-eight percent of the police sample said the most difficult situations were family disturbances. Fourteen percent cited traffic violations and drinking cases. Another 12% mentioned situations in which there were compassionate grounds for withholding the exactions of the law, as for example when a minor offense had been committed by a man with a large family. Other officers spoke of complaints where there was a lack of clear-cut evidence: for example, attempted rape or disturbing the peace.

Officers were asked to specify the most common kinds of nonenforcement situations they faced. They listed in rank order family squabbles, requests for general information, health emergencies, minor complaints involving trespassing and prowlers, recovery of bicycles, lending assistance at fires and when animals pose a threat, and behavioral problems

[12] *The Challenge of Crime in a Free Society,* p. 106.

involving children. It is quite clear that what policemen have in mind as nonenforcement contacts involve instances both in which criminal law could never be applied and in which it must be applied at the discretion of the officer.

According to the testimony of police officers, nonenforcement contacts are not concentrated among particular socioeconomic groups in the city. In fact, officers consistently testify that different socioeconomic groups present different kinds of nonenforcement problems. Officers in the sample were given a list of locations in the city and were asked to specify the kind of duty a policeman would expect to be called upon to perform at each. In their view assistance calls not involving criminal violations were most likely to come from the Dominant well-to-do parts of the city.[13] Low-income areas in which Negro or Spanish-named minorities lived were least likely to require nonenforcement assistance.[14] At the same time, officers indicate that the most ambiguous situations, situations in which the decision to apply legal sanctions is most difficult, arise in precisely those areas characterized by low incomes and high concentrations of minorities.[15] These are the areas where officers most ex-

[13] Monaco and First Avenue, Third and Franklin, Iliff and Madison.

[14] Tenth and Mariposa, Thirty-third and Arapahoe, Glencoe and Thirty-third, Nineteenth and Lawrence, Twenty-fifth and Decatur. The Glencoe and Thirty-third citation is curious. It is certainly not a low-income area, although it is solidly Negro. The Glencoe and Thirty-third address is consistently associated with other locations of high minority concentration in the responses of police officers, even though residents there enjoy higher incomes than people at the other locations. As we point out later, it is clear that ethnicity is more important than class in the perceptions of police officers.

[15] Tenth and Mariposa, Thirty-third and Arapahoe, Glencoe and Thirty-third, Twenty-fifth and Decatur.

pect to encounter family disputes and general disturbances, such as complaints of noise, parties, loiterers, and crowds. As we have already seen, these occasions, by the testimony of officers, present the most troublesome arrest decisions. In other words, in low-income minority areas policemen least expect to be called upon to give nonenforcement assistance but most expect to be confronted with complex discretionary situations. The reverse is true of Dominant middle- and upper-class areas.

It is also in Dominant well-to-do areas that policemen expect to be confronted with the clearest enforcement situations.[16] In these areas crime is against property and involves automobile accidents; application of the law is relatively straightforward. Crimes against property and involving automobiles were least expected in some of the low-income minority areas.[17] Police officers are very consistent in their testimony about what to expect at different locations in the city. We found no association whatsoever between the kinds of duty-calls officers expected from different locations and the officers' own police experience. Their expectations were unaffected by length of service, rank, nature of duty, or even area of the city to which officers were assigned. Police officers not only carry very detailed maps of the city in their minds but they evidently color these maps almost identically with respect to the kinds of behavior to expect in different locations.[18]

Other evidence obtained in the survey supports the conclusions that policemen are well aware that many, if not

[16] Third and Franklin, First and Monaco, Sixteenth and Glenarm, Iliff and Madison.

[17] Nineteenth and Lawrence, Glencoe and Thirty-third, Thirty-third and Arapahoe.

[18] This point will be explored in greater depth in the next chapter.

most, of their contacts with the public are likely not to involve enforcement and that different kinds of nonenforcement situations are more common among different kinds of people. Officers were asked to indicate what kinds of requests for assistance would come from various kinds of people. In the case of a poor or unemployed, married Negro man, 36% of the officers thought that a family problem was most likely. The next most important problem, cited by 14% of the officers, was a medical emergency. Another 14% cited a request for general information and advice. From a poor or unemployed Spanish-named married man, 32% of the officers thought a family problem was most likely to be the cause of a request for police help. Contrary to the Negro case, officers ranked medical emergencies as only the fourth most likely cause for police intervention with the poor, married Spanish-named man. Second in importance, cited by 19% of the officers, was a neighborhood disturbance, need, or problem—such as a dispute, assault, drunkenness, or violation of a city ordinance. On the other hand, from working-class Catholic parents the request most expected (30% of the officers) involved giving assistance with children —because they were lost, had been left unattended, needed counseling, or to reinforce the edicts of parents. Medical emergencies were expected by only 2% of the officers. A middle-class Jewish housewife was expected to call primarily in connection with a neighborhood problem or need, such as having the home kept under watch during a vacation, to recover stolen property, or to check for prowlers. The second most expected pretext involved theft or burglary; the third was a request for general information. Not one officer expected to be called about a health emergency. Similarly with Dominant well-to-do businessmen. Forty-nine percent of the officers said businessmen would call about an enforcement situation such as a theft or burglary. The second most likely call would involve a neighborhood problem, primarily of a security kind; the third most likely was a request for general information.

When asked to indicate which kinds of people would be most apt to make a nonenforcement demand upon the police, officers listed in order women, old people, poor people, Spanish-named, Negroes, middle-class people, businessmen, and the wealthy.

In summary, our data show that nonenforcement contacts make up the bulk of police-public contacts and that this is recognized by policemen. However, nonenforcement stems from different causes, either because the request for assistance doesn't involve a matter of law at all or because the automatic application of the law would be inappropriate or inexpedient. Policemen firmly believe that the most ambiguous nonenforcement situations involve lower-class and primarily minority people. Nonenforcement contacts among well-to-do Dominants are the result of calls for assistance involving matters extraneous to the application of legal rules. At the same time, there is one kind of clear nonenforcement request that is more prevalent among lower-class minority people, namely, the medical emergency.

Whether or not the perceptions of police officers are accurate cannot be tested satisfactorily from the data at hand. The survey of the general public did reveal that Negroes and Spanish-named persons were two to three times as likely to have called the police about a medical emergency than were Dominants. At the same time, family problems, which figure so prominently in the expectations of policemen about calls from minority neighborhoods, were only slightly more prevalent among minorities in the general public survey. Just over 2% of Dominants, 2.9% of Negroes, and 7.1% of the Spanish-named said they had called for this reason. It was not among the top four reasons listed by any ethnic group. One could understand, however, that people might be reluctant to mention domestic troubles to a stranger-interviewer, particularly if the problems were serious enough to justify calling the police. Perhaps the best way to document the kinds of demands that are actually made on the police would be by analyzing the calls recorded by the police in the dispatcher's office. Most requests for police assistance do come in by telephone or they are at least the subject of discussion over the police radio.

Since the police themselves perceive that they are functioning very largely as peace officers, the question arises as to whether they are being properly trained, organized, and directed to handle the mass of discretionary, nonenforcement contacts to which they are exposed. As the President's Commission on Law Enforcement and Criminal Justice said:

The organization of police departments and the training of policemen are focused almost entirely on the apprehension and prosecution of criminals. What a policeman does, or should do, instead of making an arrest or in order to avoid making an arrest, or in a situation in which he may not make an arrest, is rarely discussed. The peacekeeping and service activities, which consume the majority of police time, receive too little consideration.[19]

There seems to be a pervasive misunderstanding among many people about what the police do and hence how they should be trained and led. The misunderstanding is embodied in the phrase "officer of the law" or "lawman." Most tragically of all, many policemen themselves draw conclu-

[19] *The Challenge of Crime in a Free Society,* p. 92.

sions about what they should be doing from this conception, even though they are by and large honest enough—as this study shows—to realize how they are really spending their time. Even experienced police officers, such as the late Chief of the Los Angeles Police Department, William H. Parker, resist attempts to make them more conscious of human relations problems by arguing that policemen are not agents of social welfare and adjustment. Policemen, in this view, must be deployed according to criminal effects, not criminal causes.[20] This perspective beclouds the richness and complexity of police contacts in the community. It is quite true that policemen must enforce law and maintain order—that is the task laid upon them. But what is not generally perceived, or admitted, is that in meeting this obligation policemen daily engage in activities designed to prevent unambiguously criminal situations from arising and to ameliorate stressful circumstances. It would be wrong, as Parker correctly points out, to think of the police primarily as a social or welfare agency, but it would be equally wrong to fail to realize that training in amelioration and human relations may serve the officer day in and day out, in fulfillment of his formal function, as usefully as training in the use of gun, nightstick, and handcuffs.[21]

[20] W. H. Parker, "The Police Role in Community Relations," published by the National Conference of Christians and Jews, 1955, pp. 25-27.

[21] In partial recognition of this fact, Chief of Police Seaton, in one of his first official actions after appointment in December 1967 banned the routine wearing of white plastic helmets and the carrying of nightsticks in contacts with the public. These implements were to be kept in the patrol car, available if needed, but not in evidence normally. The Chief said that a "new image" of the police was needed and that the hard hats and nightsticks made policemen appear too martial. The

WILLINGNESS TO CONTACT

We have already seen that among the three major ethnic groups in Denver, the same proportion (about 23%) have called the police for help during the previous year. In discussing personal problems, however, despite the fact that minority people drew upon the services of state and municipal agencies generally more than did Dominants, a significantly smaller proportion of minority persons than Dominants utilized the police agency specifically. This seems anomalous, especially if one notes that minority people had greater reason for doing so as a result of a higher proportional incidence of involvement with the law. It seems reasonable to conclude that the factor of ethnicity is affecting the willingness of people to discuss problems with the police.

The fact that the proportion of people who called the police for help was the same in each ethnic group can also be used as presumptive evidence that minority people are less willing to request police assistance. Figures on the incidence of crime for the nation show that rates of victimization are much higher among minorities than Dominants. In fact, the risk of victimization is highest among lower-income groups generally, but especially high among the minorities.[22] The need for police help and protection is greater for minority people. One could conclude either that

---

order was immediately attacked by some people in the community, primarily on the grounds that the public, as well as the officers, were now defenseless. Their concern is without foundation. The Chief's order is a much more accurate reflection of what policemen are actually called upon to do than are statements in opposition to the order.

[22] *The Challenge of Crime in a Free Society,* p. 39.

minority people are much less alarmed by criminal dangers than Dominants or that they are less willing to seek protection by calling the police.

One item in the survey was designed to test directly whether minority groups were less willing to resort to the police. The public was asked whether they had ever thought of calling the police but then decided not to. The results showed that there were only slight differences among ethnic groups. Fifteen percent of Negroes said that they had thought of doing so and then decided against it; 17% of Dominants and 21% of Spanish-named people agreed. This is hardly overwhelming evidence of massive reluctance in the minority communities relative to the Dominants. Respondents were also asked what made them decide not to go ahead with their plan to call the police. The answers were almost identical among ethnic groups, except that minority people were more apt than Dominants to attribute their change of plan to some judgment about the police. For instance, 14.3% of the Dominants who changed their minds did so because they thought the police were too slow, inefficient, or useless. Among Negroes who changed their minds, 30% gave this as a reason; and among Spanish-named people, 26.3%.[23] So there is some evidence that reluctance among minority communities can be traced to feelings about the police.

Analysis of the data shows no association between deciding not to call the police and characteristics of socioeconomic status. Within each ethnic group, there is no linkage between class and reluctance to call the police. We may conclude, on the basis of this survey item, that if reluctance

[23] It should be noted, however, that the size of the subsamples was forty-nine in the case of Dominants, thirty-three for Negroes, and thirty-eight for Spanish-named. These are not large samples.

to call the police exists, it is a function of ethnicity and not of social class.

People are not always demanding something of the police when they have contact with them; there is a dimension of sociable contact which importantly supplements contacts that fall within the line of a policeman's duty. For example, policemen often note that people like to know policemen and like to stop an officer to talk, to kid around, or to pass the time of day. In fact 45% of the officers interviewed said this occurred "quite frequently." Another 29% said that it happened "fairly frequently." Twenty-two percent said that it was rare. The vast majority of policemen, therefore, accept sociable contacts of an informal nature as being part of the job. Among members of the public, about four out of ten said they have had a friendly talk with a policeman. However, there is an important difference between Spanish-named people and everyone else (see Table 3-4). Whereas 46% of Dominants and 45% of Negroes have had a friendly talk with policemen, only 33% of Spanish-

TABLE 3—4

WHETHER OR NOT MEMBERS OF MAJORITY AND MINORITY GROUPS IN THE GENERAL PUBLIC EVER HAD A FRIENDLY TALK WITH POLICEMEN WHO WORK IN THEIR NEIGHBORHOOD

Whether or Not They Ever Had a Friendly Talk with Policemen Who Work in Their Neighborhoods	MAJORITY		MINORITY GROUPS			
	Dominants	%	Negroes	%	Spanish	%
Yes	156	46	106	45	77	33
No	178	53	130	55	154	66
Don't recall	1	0	0	0	0	0
Total	335	99*	236	100†	231	99‡

* One did not respond.   † Three, or 1%, did not respond.

named people have. This conforms to the finding that half as many Spanish-named people as Negroes have had a discussion with the police in the previous year about some problem or difficulty. We also saw that more Spanish-named people than Dominants or Negroes had thought of calling the police and then decided against it. One may conclude that there is somewhat greater alienation between the Spanish-named and the police than between Negroes and the police. This finding will be further investigated in Chapter 5.

There is no indication that class status affects the likelihood of having a friendly talk with policemen.

The public was also asked whether they had any personal acquaintances among policemen generally or in their neighborhood particularly. At least one-third of the public claimed to have a personal acquaintance on the force and about half of these said that these are either close personal friends or relatives. Among the ethnic groups, the proportions with personal acquaintances on the force were 38% among Dominants, 41% among Negroes, and 31% among Spanish-named. Interestingly, fewer people personally knew policemen who were stationed in their own neighborhood. Among Dominants the proportion was 9%, among Negroes 13%, and among Spanish-named 11%. It does not appear that people become acquainted with policemen primarily due to proximity. Although one cannot determine the closeness of these relationships, the data suggest that from the point of view of the public, policemen in a given neighborhood are not closer to its people on a personal basis than policemen stationed any other place. These facts persuasively support the notion that assignment of policemen to a particular area does not mean that they will develop personal relationships with people of the neighborhood. The day when the cop on the beat knew everyone and everyone knew him seems to have passed.

Analysis also shows that ethnicity importantly affects whom the public becomes personally acquainted with on the force. Among Dominants who said they were personally acquainted with a policeman working in the neighborhood, not one of them said that his police acquaintance was either Negro or Spanish. It may be true, of course, that given the few minority officers on the Denver force, assignment policy has concentrated them in minority areas. There would be, therefore, less opportunity for Dominant contacts with minority policemen. The evidence from minority members of the public indicates that something besides assignment policy is at work. Among Negroes who have a personal acquaintance on the force in the neighborhood, 4% said the policemen were Dominant and 6% said they were Negro. None of them said they were Spanish-named. Among Spanish-named people, 7% had police acquaintances who were Dominants, 6% had some who were Spanish-named, and not one had any who were Negro. These figures demonstrate graphically that recruitment of minority policemen has not yet affected patterns of personal relation between the Dominant and minority communities and that ethnic distinctions are made among minority groups as far as personal associations are concerned.

Relations between public and police are sufficiently close that about one-quarter of all respondents said someone in the police department had done what the respondent considered to be a personal favor for them.[24]

[24] The proportions were 25% among Dominants, 21% among Negroes, and 24% among the Spanish-named.

Our data indicate that policemen are not entirely face-
less functionaries. A substantial portion of the population,
although not a majority, is able to identify a policeman as
a personal acquaintance. Moreover, almost as substantial a
portion of the population has reason to feel that someone
on the force has done him a personal favor. If, therefore,
one adds personal contacts to line-of-duty contacts, about
55% of the adult population has had contact of some sort
with a policeman in a given year.[25]

Although Spanish-named people seem less willing than
other people to make use of the police and to have a friendly
talk with them, there are no important differences among
ethnic groups with respect to the proportion of them that
have personal acquaintances on the force. The potential for
social contacts with policemen seems to be the same across
ethnic lines.

CONCLUSION

In the Denver community, which is probably not atypical among urban areas, as many as 55% of the adult community has had some contact with the police in the course of
a year. While some of these contacts are not in the line
of duty—they are informal sociable contacts—more than half
of them occur when the citizen believes he has a pressing

[25] In making this calculation allowance has been made for the fact
that there is some overlap between categories. That is, some people
who have had line-of-duty contact also have had sociable contact.
Analysis does show that people with a personal acquaintance on the
force are more likely than others to have called the police for help or
to have discussed a problem with them. The chi-square values for this
association were significant at the 5% level for all ethnic groups.

need requiring police attention. These are situations in which the quality of police response is likely to be remembered. One must never forget that policemen interact with people at times of great stress and emotional crisis. Public contacts with policemen, unlike those with most other municipal employees, are not likely to be routine. As the President's Commission on Law Enforcement and Criminal Justice has put it:

It is hard to overestimate the intimacy of the contact between the police and the community. Policemen deal with people when they are both most threatening and most vulnerable, when they are angry, when they are frightened, when they are desperate, when they are drunk, when they are violent, or when they are ashamed.[26]

Ethnicity, not class, seems to affect the number of contacts with the police. Negroes and Spanish-named persons are less likely to have had a significant contact with the police than are Dominants both relative to their needs and relative to the demands they make upon all governmental agencies. Utilization of the police figures more largely in the world of the Dominant citizen than of the minority citizen. Our study has provided presumptive, but not direct, evidence that minority people are more reluctant to call upon the police than Dominants and that the reason for their reluctance stems from the belief that the police cannot or will not help them. Moreover, Spanish-named people tend to be less willing to become involved with the police than Negroes.

Although police contacts with the public are likely to be fraught with emotion, they are not likely to involve either arrest or the issuance of a citation. Punitive aspects

[26] *The Challenge of Crime in a Free Society,* p. 91.

of law enforcement are evident in only a small proportion of contacts. The vast majority of contacts involve the police in rendering assistance, with no question of applying criminal statutes, or in interceding so as to avoid the occurrence of a situation in which arrest would be mandatory. In the eyes of the police different segments of the population present the officer with different kinds of nonenforcement situations. For nonminority middle- or upper-class people, officers expect nonenforcement contact to involve pure calls for assistance. From minority and lower-class people nonenforcement calls are likely to be highly discretionary, involving family disputes and neighborhood altercations. The only nonenforcement assistance call that comes much more regularly from disadvantaged people concerns health emergencies, where the police are expected to determine whether professional medical attention is needed.

The testimony of Denver policemen demonstrates conclusively that policemen spend most of their time acting more as "peace officers" than "law officers." Although they must be prepared to apprehend the dangerous criminal, they will in fact devote more of their energy to nonenforcement contacts with the public, often involving the making of harrowing decisions about the appropriateness of making an arrest.

chapter 4

The
Policeman's
World

Being a member of an occupation entails viewing the world from a particular perspective. Quite simply, people become sensitized to the existence of a particular gamut of problems. They become more aware of certain aspects of their environmnt and overlook others. But occupational affiliations do more than sensitize people to particular facets of life. They also provide rough-and-ready evaluative categories concerning the nature of the problems encountered and the operational requirements for their solution. Thus an experienced doctor is not only more aware than the layman that people are ill; he makes impressionistic judgments about how ill they might be, what the illness is, and how important it would be for them to seek medical help. Occupational affiliation carries with it models, perhaps more accurately, templates, which people can apply to situations in order to make initial judgments relevant to meeting the situations to which they have become attuned. The act of belonging to an occupation, then, serves to impose meaning upon the myriad impressions from the everyday world. In an important sense the perceptual world a person inhabits is affected, perhaps determined in large measure, by the nature of the work he chooses to do. And his behavior, especially as it is related to his calling, will be critically influenced by the interpretive rules which are the inherited wisdom of his particular occupation.

So it is with policemen. What policemen do is a function in some degree of what they are asked to do and what they, out of the collective experience of the profession, believe are salient aspects of their environment. If one is to understand why policemen do as they do, it is essential to comprehend the world they have learned to live in. It is also essential to understand what evaluations are considered of elementary and practical significance in accomplishing the tasks demanded of them. This chapter explores the policeman's perceptual world, focusing especially on the behavioral cues to which the policeman is alert and which provide basic information relevant to the making of decisions.

CUES TO DANGER

Policemen are attuned to the defense of life and property. Their primary charge, as they see it, is to protect the community from the depredations of persons who are criminal, disorderly, or thoughtless. Their professional mandate is to prevent such occurrences and to apprehend the people so engaged. Through their training and their association with fellow officers they become alerted to circumstances linked with criminal trouble. To lay observers of police work, police sensitivity to seemingly innocuous details is both impressive and uncanny. On night patrol, for example, policemen will note that their headlights have not reflected off a pane of glass in a warehouse window. This means a broken pane, possibly the result of breaking and entering. A car parked near a used-car lot late at night containing a sole occupant could be a "lookout" for a car-stripping gang. A seedy man carrying a brown-paper parcel through a well-to-do neighborhood could be a burglar. He might also be lost or on his way home from work, but in any case the policeman may feel compelled to investigate. A policeman's world is filled with cues spelling potential danger to the community; the policeman will use his authority to determine whether the danger is real. Indeed, were he not hypersensitive to the possibility of criminal activity, he would be derelict in his duty and the community, as well as his superiors, would censure him severely. Is it possible to make any generalizations about the perceptual cues that trigger the attention of policemen?

The previous chapter has indicated that policemen, with remarkable agreement, expect to be used in rather different ways in different parts of the city. By and large they expect to be presented with the clearest enforcement cases, unambiguous criminal events, in the middle- and upper-class area and the business and commercial sections of the city. The most discretionary situations, however, occur in the poor and minority residential areas. Tabulating the expectations of policemen about the likelihood of different crimes in various parts of the city, we find that they consider crimes against property most common in the middle- and upper-class sections of the city.[1] Crimes against persons, such as assaults, shootings, and fighting, are considered by policemen to be most common in the lower-class and minority areas. Unlike crimes against property, crimes against persons are considered least common in the well-to-do, nonminority parts of the city.[2] It seems reasonable to infer that policemen are put more on their mettle in lower-class, minority neighborhoods than in well-to-do nonminority areas. Although the apprehension of any criminal is hazardous, whether the crime has been against persons or property, policemen associate patrol in disadvantaged areas with a high amount of discretionary intervention and the possibility of violence against persons. These are the kinds of situations where danger to the police officer may erupt without warning. He feels that he must be more alert to the unexpected and especially to the sudden surge of passion that precipitates an attack upon himself. By contrast, in well-to-do areas the nature of the crime is likely to be more clear and the policeman feels he is the hunter and not the hunted. Furthermore, he will not have to deal with masses of people, unsure of himself as to who is at fault.[3]

The greater danger perceived in police work in disadvantaged neighborhoods is graphically demonstrated by

[1] In order, Third and Franklin, Sixteenth and Glenarm, First and Monaco, Iliff and Madison, while last on the list are Tenth and Mariposa, Thirty-third and Arapahoe, and Glencoe and Thirty-third.

[2] Policemen considered crimes against persons to be most likely at Tenth and Mariposa, Thirty-third and Arapahoe, Glencoe and Thirty-third, and Twenty-fifth and Decatur; least likely at Monaco and First, Third and Franklin, and Iliff and Madison.

[3] It is worth noting that in *Field Survey* 3, Vol. II, p. 21, prepared for the President's Commission on Law Enforcement and Criminal Justice, the authors found that in the typical contact situation more

answers to another survey question. Policemen were asked in what locations in Denver they thought resistance in making an arrest was most likely to be found, regardless of the nature of the offense. Policemen listed the minority and economically depressed areas first and the middle- and upper-class Dominant areas last.[4] It is particularly interesting that the Negro middle-class location was included among those where resistance was thought to be most likely, while the lower middle-class Dominant area was included at the top of the list of areas where resistance was least expected.[5] There seems little doubt that interpersonal violence as well as violence directed against policemen is considered more likely to take place in minority neighborhoods regardless of economic class. Anxiety levels among officers are likely to be higher, therefore, in minority areas than in any other parts of the city.

An officer's view of what he will be called upon to do at any particular location is affected by his experience as a policeman. We find an association between his expectations, on the one hand, and the nature of his duty, the location of his assignment, and the number of years he has served on the force, on the other.[6] These results would indicate

---

people were involved per encounter with Negroes than with Dominants. The authors concluded that officers are faced with greater problems of control in contacts with Negroes. Our evidence supports this conclusion, and also shows that policemen are aware of this factor.

[4] Tenth and Mariposa, Thirty-third and Arapahoe, Glencoe and Thirty-third versus Third and Franklin, Monaco and First, Iliff and Madison, Quitman and West Second.

[5] Glencoe and Thirty-third versus Quitman and West Second.

[6] Chi-square values were significant at better than the 5% level and most were better than the 1% level. There were ten locations in Denver specified for the officer to evaluate. Nature of duty was correlative with eight of them; location of assignment with six of them; and years on the force with seven of them.

that experience is a teacher of policemen; they do not all hold exactly the same views about what kinds of situations they will be required to face in different socioeconomic neighborhoods in Denver. On the other hand, there are not significant correlations of this kind with officers' expectations about whether resistance is likely to be encountered in an arrest. Since officers are in complete agreement as well about the areas in Denver which are either most supporting of or hostile toward the police, as pointed out in Chapter 2, the conclusion is that experience on the job affects views about the requirements of different neighborhoods, but it does not affect more evaluative judgments touching upon the quality of relations between police and public in contact situations.

It is almost impossible to obtain a definitive list of cues which alert police officers to criminal activity. There are as many cues as there are crimes. It is apparent also that cues vary with location and situation. Circumstances that arouse suspicion in one place and one social context do not do so in another. A shaggy-headed young man in dirty boots and levis carrying a bag of tools would attract scarcely a glance around the Denver Coliseum, but the same man would probably be stopped and questioned if he appeared late at night in a prosperous residential area. Policemen were asked to specify cues of manner and dress that did alert them to possible criminal activity. One theme recurred again and again in their answers: they looked for inappropriateness of dress or an unusual manner. In short, they looked for incongruity. Their answers indicate that they are attuned both to measuring people against the immediate environment and drawing conclusions about whether the persons fit against that background. For example, the suspicions of a policeman may be raised by the following situations: a man wearing an overcoat on a hot day, persons loitering where children play, unescorted young women in public places late at night, shabby people in prosperous neighborhoods or well-dressed people in run-down neighborhoods, parked couples in industrial areas, and people who show exaggerated unconcern about the presence of a police officer or who try to evade the officer.[7]

What is important to realize is that measuring people against their surrounding is an essential part of police activity. A policeman is chronically suspicious and he is forced, by the nature of the duty with which he is entrusted, to make snap decisions about the appropriateness of what people are doing. Since he is looking for the unusual, his decisions are environment-specific; what action he takes depends upon what is perceived to be common for that area. The fact that policemen are alert for incongruity probably does militate against minority persons. Policemen do believe crime emanates from the disadvantaged more commonly than from members of the Dominant or well-to-do community. Furthermore, due to the geography of American cities there is simply more opportunity, indeed necessity, for minority people and the poor to enter surroundings in which they appear incongruous. Living in a middle-class society dominated by whites, Negroes especially, and the poor as well, are likely to appear "out of place" more often than others. They not only are more "visible" to policemen by virtue of their expected association with crime, but they have more opportunity to be "visible." This being the case,

[7] Some of these points appear in an article by Thomas F. Adams, "Field Interrogation," *Police*, (March-April 1963), 28. Quoted by Skolnick, *op. cit.*, pp. 45-46, footnote.

it is probable, although our study did not test it directly, that minority people and the poor do attract more police suspicion than nonminority, prosperous people.

Policemen are also more alert to certain kinds of potential crimes than to others because of the seriousness they attach to them. These value judgments color their perceptual world too and encourage them to become more attentive to certain circumstances. In the survey policemen were asked to indicate, from a list given them, the crimes they considered most serious. In decreasing order of seriousness, they listed the following: sexual molestation of a minor, rape, drug passing, assaulting an officer, robbery, child neglect, rioting, drug addiction, assault, burglary, looting, sexual deviance, auto theft, speeding in a motor vehicle, disturbing the peace, prostitution, and drunkenness. The ranking given by Denver policemen conforms to that found in other studies,[8] except that Denver policemen put sexual deviance considerably farther down the list. It would appear that Denver policemen tend to think of sexual deviance more as a vice, like prostitution and drunkenness, than as a serious criminal offense.

The behavior of police officers is particularly affected by their perception of the danger to themselves. The greater their anxiety, the less likely they will be to take chances, the more likely they will be to demand that events run as they think they should, and the quicker they will be to act to forestall injury to themselves. There is no question that policemen are more anxious in minority neighborhoods than any place else. Asked to indicate in which locations they most expected to encounter antagonistic and hostile response to them, policemen put the minority areas at the

[8] See Niederhoffer, *op. cit.*, pp. 122-123.

top of the list.[9] The middle- and upper-class Dominant areas were labeled most cooperative and helpful and least antagonistic and hostile. Once again the middle-class Negro area was included among the areas where hostility was most likely to be encountered. Race is undoubtedly an important perceptual cue for policemen when they gauge the possibility of harm coming to themselves.

Policemen have personal evidence for the need to be concerned about public response. Ninety-eight of them claim they have been abused on some occasion, either physically or verbally. While the proportion of officers who report to have experienced abuse in some form does not vary with the nature or location of their assignment, officers who assert they have been *physically* abused (as opposed to being verbally abused) are more likely to be assigned at the time of the interview to a police district with a high proportion of minority people.[10] For example, nineteen officers said that they were on fixed assignment to a police district and that they have been physically abused. Five of these were assigned to District 1, seven to District 2. These two districts contain the bulk of Denver's minority population; District 2 is heavily Negro. The other three districts accounted for the other seven officers who had been abused. Thus, of those officers who claimed to have been physically abused, more of them were assigned to minority neighborhoods than to nonminority ones. These statistics are deceptive, however. The proportion of officers assigned to these two districts is greater than to others. Analysis does *not* show that among

[9] In descending order; Glencoe and Thirty-third, Thirty-third and Arapahoe, Tenth and Mariposa, Nineteenth and Lawrence, Twenty-fifth and Decatur.

[10] The chi-square value was significant between the 2% and 5% levels.

all officers assigned to any district the proportion of physical to verbal abuse is greater in minority group districts. In short, among officers who have been physically abused, most of them are likely to have had the experience in a minority neighborhood. From this one might draw the conclusion that physical abuse is more common there. That is true, but the number of patrolmen—and presumably of contacts—is also greater there. For any particular policeman assigned to a minority area, the likelihood of his experiencing physical abuse is no greater than if he were assigned any place else. On the basis of our evidence we would be as justified in concluding that physical abuse is as much a function of the number of policemen as it is of the ethnic character of the neighborhood. Since greater numbers of policemen are assigned to minority group districts, one cannot tell whether it is the neighborhood or the policemen that cause the greater incidence of physical abuse in these districts.

The testimony of so many men, however, who happen to be assigned to minority areas, probably helps to create a climate of opinion against that neighborhood. A police officer on the force would meet more fellow officers who had been physically abused in minority areas than elsewhere. And he would not have the data to know that the *proportion* of physical to verbal abuse in the minority neighborhoods is *not* greater than elsewhere.

There can be little doubt that policemen are sensitized to minority people. As we have seen, there are several reasons why police think this: they believe that the involvement of minorities with crime is greater than for other ethnic groups; that minorities involve policemen in mediating very ambiguous and very emotional human situations, and not infrequently involving crimes against persons;

that hostility toward policemen is greater among minority people, particularly in the form of resisting arrest; and that physical attacks on officers are more common in these areas than elsewhere, for which they think they have firsthand testimony.

Expectations about public behavior is a function of occupational demands and socialization. Policemen certainly share with one another views about the likelihood of different kinds of behavior. Our analysis has shown that views among officers are remarkably homogeneous. At the same time, it is possible that views about what to expect are a function to some extent of the kind of people policemen are. In an attempt to answer this question, we correlated items dealing with the personality and background of policemen with their views about what to expect in the community. We found only inconsistent and fragmentary associations. This is especially important for the factors of personality. Our analysis leads us to conclude that, subject to the reliability and sensitivity of our survey instrument, the expectations of policemen about what they will encounter in the way of behavior among different sections of the population are not a function of particular personality or sociological characteristics of the officers.

The element of danger is something that policemen live with daily. They are trained from the beginning in self-defense and in the use of weapons. Our study has shown that about a third of all Denver's policemen report they have been physically attacked or shot at. Policemen are the community's foremost defense against violence, whether committed by individuals or groups. They do stand as a thin blue line between the citizen and those people choosing to flaunt society's norms and values. This being the case,

it is easy to see how policemen become sensitized to the possibility of danger, partly as a normal human reaction, partly
because duty enjoins them to meet and contain it.

During our survey policemen were shown a hand-drawn
sketch of an officer stepping out of his patrol car and
approaching a casually dressed young man who had his
hands in his pockets. When officers were asked during the
interview what they thought the policeman was thinking,
34%—double the next largest response—said the officer was
wondering what the man had in his pocket.

Every year the FBI presents statistics about the number of officers assaulted and killed in the line of duty. In
1966, for example, slightly over one out of every ten officers
were assaulted.[11] There is some evidence, however, that the
element of physical danger in police work has been over-
stated. A task force studying the police, operating under the
aegis of the President's Commission on Law Enforcement
and Criminal Justice, noted that the most recent study of
deaths in various occupations—1955—showed that the rate
of police fatalities while on duty, and including accidents,
was 33 per 100,000 officers, which was less than the rate for
mining, agriculture, construction, and transportation.[12]
Using the FBI's figures of 99 deaths of police officers in
1966 and a total law-enforcement establishment of 272,659[13]
the rate is 36.2 per 100,000.

The emphasis upon danger in police work, while it
cannot be neglected entirely, can perhaps be reduced so as
to conform more accurately with the operational require-

[11] Federal Bureau of Investigation, *Uniform Crime Reports—1966,*
p. 152.

[12] *Task Force Report: The Police,* p. 189.

[13] Including sheriffs' departments and suburban police forces.

ments of the job. At the same time, it would be naive, in our view, to believe that policemen will not remain concerned and anxious about the dangerous nature of their work and that their behavior will not be affected by it. The fact is that, like military personnel, policemen are killed or hurt in the line of duty for the sake of the wider community; they face danger in order to protect the rest of us. We demand, as it were, that they risk their lives. This is not true of other occupations. Even more important, the danger policemen face is not impersonal; it is not a mechanistic act of God, as when a flood occurs, a building collapses, or a fire breaks out. It is an act of man upon man, and somehow this kind of violence seems particularly abhorrent to the public and police alike. Therefore, because of the real danger the job entails and because of the psychological importance of the kind of danger policemen face, it is doubtful if policemen will not continue to be preternaturally alert to behavioral clues indicating danger, and that their activities in the community will not be profoundly affected by deeply held opinions about which kinds of people can be trusted.

INHIBITING FACTORS

When policemen move into the city on patrol they are alert to various cues that spell danger to themselves or the community. But this is only part of the story. They also carry with them expectations about the potential threat of different kinds of people and situations upon their own careers. Since policemen, like most people gainfully employed, want to safeguard as well as advance their careers, officers are affected by what they foresee as the repercussions flowing from their activity upon their standing with superiors and the wider community.

Policemen want to appear to discharge their work responsibly and ably without attracting undue notoriety and controversy. They want to do their work and stay out of trouble. A policeman's every instinct is for anonymity. Not, of course, among his peers, but certainly among the public. After all, his whole purpose is to maintain peace, harmony, and order in the community. If his intercession does not result in a more stable and calm situation, he has failed in his job. A policeman's guiding imperative is to quiet things down. If he must make an arrest, he wants to do so in the least disruptive way. Indeed, policemen get reputations among fellow officers for being unable to make an unobtrusive arrest. The officer who gets embroiled in an unruly public scene attracts a good deal of derisive humor from his colleagues. If a man shows himself chronically unable to intercede without raising emotions to a higher level, the fact is noted by his superiors. Officers may be cautioned or moved to other jobs if they do not have the gift of anonymous intervention. One of the important norms of police work is, then, to keep the lid on situations with the least amount of public violence. And, it is tacitly understood among policemen that what happens during a contact depends overwhelmingly upon the demeanor of the officer. As will be shown later,[14] there is a corollary to this. When force is deemed necessary, it must be used effectively. That is, it must produce the required results in short order; halfway measures will not do.

There are certain kinds of situations and certain kinds

[14] Chapter 7.

of people that spell trouble for a policeman. The first among these are women, especially female drunks. Asked to specify the kinds of people they would rather *not* be faced with arresting, officers listed women, drug addicts, drunks, mental cases, parents in domestic disputes, and affluent and influential people, such as lawyers, politicians, doctors, and opinion-leaders. It is clear that different inhibiting considerations are involved in each case. For policemen the sex of a woman is a potent weapon of defense. The use of force against women is distasteful to policemen, and it is likely to arouse public indignation as well. Furthermore, they are dreadfully sensitive to the charge of sexual molestation. When Denver officers pick up a woman, they are required to radio to the dispatcher the time of pickup and the mileage of the patrol car's speedometer. When they arrive at their destination, commonly the county jail or a police office, they report the time of arrival and once again the mileage. These reports are a protection for them, being evidence that the officer took a reasonably direct route and a reasonable length of time. Officers lumped women together with drug addicts, drunks, and mental cases as being the "worst" kinds of arrests to make. The latter three kinds are unpredictable, sometimes vicious, and often dirty and foul. The third category of distasteful arrests involves people in domestic disturbances. Domestic disturbances are considered by officers to be the most difficult situations from the point of view of whether an arrest should be made. Policemen indicate, as well, that making an arrest in an emotional domestic entanglement is likely to lead to a renewed outbreak of passion. If children are involved, the policeman must take steps to provide care for the children until the parents are released. All in all, these sticky situations play upon the sympathies of policemen, the vast majority of whom are staunch family men themselves. A very different range of considerations must account for the reluctance policemen feel about arresting people who are powerful and influential. In this case, the potential threat is to their own careers. They feel uneasy that these people might be able to outpoint them with their superiors or with others in the upper reaches of municipal government.

Class status very clearly carries with it, in the minds of policemen, an implied threat. Police officers know that the higher the class of the complainant, especially if Dominant, the greater the likelihood that he will appeal over the officer's head. We asked policemen to indicate the locations in Denver where they thought it most likely that they would be threatened with an appeal over their heads. Far and away the most likely location was the wealthy section of Monaco and First Avenue, associated in the public mind with a relatively high concentration of Jews and professional people. This location outscored all others by over two to one. The next most likely location was another very prosperous area not far from a prestigious country club.[15] Then, very close in ranking, came the Negro locations, one of them very poor economically, the other middle-class.[16] After them came a middle-class white area and a depressed Spanish-named area. At the bottom of the list were downtown commercial areas, one of them well-to-do, the other depresssed, and a lower-middle-class area by and large Dominant but with a sprinkling of Spanish-named people. The answers to this survey question indicate only those

[15] Third and Franklin.
[16] Thirty-third and Arapahoe and Glencoe and Thirty-third, respectively.

areas where policemen *thought* the threat of an appeal against them most likely; they do not reveal whether the policemen thought the threats in each case were likely to be acted upon. Nonetheless, we can infer from this ranking that among policemen a rather sophisticated belligerency is associated with high-class rank, with professional standing, and with Negroes. It may attach to Jews as well; it is linked very little with Spanish-named people.

Another inhibiting factor is the possibility of being sued. A civil suit constitutes a threat to the policeman in two ways: first, directly upon his livelihood and, second, through the publicity and detailed examination given to his every action. The latter is probably the more powerful deterrent. Although policemen may be sued personally in Denver, damages awarded against them will be covered by insurance the city maintains for them.[17] As long as the officer has been acting conscientiously in the course of duty, the only penalties that can attach to him personally are criminal or departmental. Very few people like having their professional activity minutely scrutinized; this is as true of college professors, doctors, and lawyers as it is of policemen. Unless they are unusually self-reliant and confident, they are afraid that they may be discovered to be inadequate in ways they never dreamed of. This is particularly true when people are dealing in highly complex human relationships

[17] In fact, the situation is changing. Denver policemen had liability insurance until 1967. An amendment to the Charter of the City and County of Denver was passed which they thought conferred immunity upon them. For technical reasons, the amendment did not in fact protect them. Denver policemen in early 1968, therefore, when this study was written, were uncovered either by an immunity-granting statute or liability insurance. The Denver department was trying to obtain new liability insurance.

where there are no straightforward right or wrong courses of action. Policemen, who are apt to feel that any publicity is a mark of failure, are doubly defensive about having their decisions, frequently made in the heat of a moment, subjected to clinical study by judges and lawyers sitting in the antiseptic world of the courtroom.

Concern about being sued is palpable among Denver policemen. Almost a third of them said that they worried "a lot" about being sued. Another 41% said they were worried about it "a little," as opposed to not being worried about it at all. Slightly over a fifth of all officers have actually been sued (22%). If our sample is representative, as we think it is, this means that about 180 officers have been sued out of a force of approximately 820 men. It should be underscored unequivocally, however, that the vast majority of Denver police officers have not been sued. With one important exception analysis shows no association between background variables—such as nature of an officer's duty, location of assignment, social conservatism, political predispositions, and personality—and being sued. The single exception was that the higher an officer scored on the belligerency scale the more likely he was to have been sued.[18] The belligerency scale[19] tested the pugnaciousness of the individual or, conversely, the extent to which he was un-

[18] The chi-square value was significant between the 2% and 5% levels.

[19] The following five items constituted the belligerency scale: (1) You can't make friends with people who don't like you to begin with; (2) Trying to make up with people after a fight is just showing how weak you are; (3) When someone has done something to hurt you, you should always pay him back the same way; (4) It is better to die like a lion than live like a dog; (5) Doing favors for people who aren't about to do favors for you is a waste of time. Respondents were asked to Agree Strongly, Agree, Do Neither, Disagree, Disagree Strongly with the statements.

assertive and likely to "turn the other cheek." The fact that our measure of belligerency was crude and still turned up a significant correlation with being sued suggests, first, that the personality of the officer is a very important variable in contact situations—as most police officers recognize—and second, that people responsible for recruiting police officers should give careful attention to the value of using discriminating personality tests in the selection process.

The survey shows that officers consider the possibility of being sued to be almost three times as likely in the minority neighborhoods as anywhere else.[20] It was considered least likely downtown and among the white middle- and upper-classes. Of all the non-minority areas the very well-to-do area around Monaco and 1st Avenue, in which there is a high concentration of Jews, ranked highest.

Our study has shown that policemen differentiate among people with respect to whether they are likely to pose a threat to their careers by making contact difficult or by exposing them to censure. That such facts as we have noted do influence behavior seems reasonable; how much they influence behavior is almost impossible to say. If they do inhibit the range of an officer's action by engendering wariness, then they would confer a margin of immunity upon women, Negroes, and influential persons above all others. In the case of women, impressionistic testimony by policemen indicates that they go to great lengths not to arrest women and, if they do, to avoid the use of force. With influential members of the nonminority community, one would naturally expect a great amount of circumspection. Our survey merely bears out the supposition that policemen are attuned to the possibility of influence being

[20] Glencoe and Thirty-third, Tenth and Mariposa, Thirty-third and Arapahoe.

wielded. The effects of the threat by Negroes of suing or complaining to an officer's superiors are less easy to evaluate. Officers may consider the threat credible or they may not. We have no reason to believe that policemen would consider the threat any less real from Negroes than from women or influential persons. Moreover, we do know that officers are concerned about being sued and that they are discriminating enough in their judgments to distinguish between Negroes and Spanish-named persons in this respect.

One lesson can be drawn. Our data provide support for the proposition that, if one's object is to inhibit the police officer, then the ability and willingness to make trouble for an officer is a powerful weapon. People who can rip the veil of anonymity from the officer may make him move more cautiously. We are reasonably sure this works for women and influential persons. Is there any reason to suppose that it does not work, or cannot work, for Negroes or the Spanish-named?

CONCLUSION

Our study demonstrates that policemen live in a particular perceptual world—a cop's world, if you will. This perceptual world is common to all police officers regardless of social background, personality, years on the force, nature of duty, or location of assignment. Policemen share a set of expectations about human behavior, which they carry into professional contacts, precisely because they are policemen. Their occupation engenders a particular way of looking at their environment.

For a variety of reasons police officers are wary of minority group persons, who are also commonly disadvantaged economically, and of the areas of the city these persons inhabit. Policemen approach minority group members cautiously—alert for danger. The factor of race is clearly a specific cue in the policeman's world. Policemen associate minority status with a high incidence of crime, especially crimes against the person, with bodily harm to police officers, and with a general lack of support for the police. But minority people are also peculiarly visible to policemen because of the way in which policemen think. Policemen are attuned to incongruity, a judgment which involves fitting people against their immediate surroundings. Incongruity is the ground for a policeman's suspicions. Because they are minority people, they are bound to appear discordant to policemen in most of the environment of a middle-class, white society. For this reason they doubly draw the attention of police officers.

Negroes, much more than the Spanish-named, threaten policemen in another important way. Negroes are not acquiescent, and in this they are like members of the prosperous, influential, Dominant segment of the community. Policemen expect minority people not only to be involved in the most dangerous and demanding situations policemen must face, but to be least charitable in their judgments about what is done. Police officers believe that Negroes will try to threaten policemen indirectly, but no less effectively, by seeking publicity, by filing an action in court, and by seeking the mediation of higher authority.

Considering the expectations policemen have about what is likely from minority people, it seems plausible to expect that they might build up an enormous amount of resentment against them. The middle-class and upper-class

Dominant community, constituting the majority of people in the city, are seen by policemen as being cooperative, making straightforward demands involving little risk to the officer, and frequently requiring no enforcement at all. At the same time, these people are familiar with avenues of redress and not unwilling to challenge the officer who they believe presumes too far. Nonetheless, since their demands are generally not exorbitant from the point of view of the officer, policemen may not mind becoming unassuming, informal, polite, and even deferential in their presence. Minorities, on the other hand, especially Negroes, in the eyes of police personnel, demand the most, raise the greatest amount of anxiety about personal safety, pose the greatest criminal threat, are the most hostile, and on top of it all are as likely to be truculent in their appeals against officers as prosperous Dominants. We have only impressionistic evidence that these perceptions on the part of policemen add up to a growing feeling of resentment, but it would not be surprising if this were the case. One can understand why policemen often show a sense of being aggrieved, mistreated, and put-upon my minorities. Minorities react in an exactly similar fashion against members of the majority community. There seems to be a reciprocating engine of resentment at work in the relations between police and minorities, an engine which is fueled with the demands each side makes on the other and the expectations each entertains about the other. If police-community relations are to be improved, the nature of this relationship—and especially of the structural basis for it—must be understood and studied in great detail.

5

Minorities Confront the Police

Police-community relations are a topic of importance in contemporary America not because the entire community is alienated, distrustful, and belligerent with respect to the police but because particular groups within it are. These groups are the minority groups, especially Negroes. The burden of a great deal of reportage about the life of Negroes is that the police are a very visible, a very salient part of their everyday environment. The police seem to play a role in the life of minority people out of all proportion to the role they play in the lives of the Dominant majority. What is more, the violent riots that have dramatized the smouldering dissatisfaction of minority people—and which have threatened the complacent world of the Dominant majority —have had as their ostensible cause police contacts with minorities.

One of the primary goals of the Denver study was to determine the position occupied by the police in the world of the minority communities. This chapter attempts to view the police through minority eyeglasses, exploring the experiences minority people have had with the police and the governing attitudes they bring to contacts with policemen. Confrontation is, of course, a two-way process. The quality of the relationship is affected by the perspectives, expectations, and attitudes of policemen as well. The next chapter will therefore examine the way minorities appear through police eyeglasses. By understanding mutual perspectives, it should be possible to determine why relations have developed as they have and to project the limits within which today's strained relationship between police and minorities may be ameliorated. Hopefully the reader will be in a position to evaluate the extent to which proposed solutions to the problem of police-minority relations can produce a happier state of affairs.

MINORITY VIEWS OF THE POLICE

There is no doubt at all that minorities in Denver hold the police in less favorable regard than does the Dominant community. Negroes and the Spanish-named do not disagree with Dominants very much about the importance of police to the community, although they are not quite as convinced. Slightly more than four out of ten Dominants thought the job of policeman much more important than other jobs. Slightly more than three out of ten Negroes shared this view. Spanish-named people agreed in equal proportions with the Dominants. On the general issue of respect for the police, Spanish-named people tended to agree with the evaluations of Dominants, while Negroes were more inclined to believe that people were losing respect for the police and to be less convinced that Denver policemen enjoyed more respect than the police in other cities. It is important to note that minority members on general questions such as this are not forthrightly critical in much greater proportions than Dominants; rather, they have more in-between opinions. Their opinions are poised between praise and blame. The Dominants, on the other hand, are more willing to praise. The more adverse minority comments about the police showed up on questions asking for an evaluation of police performance in the immediate neighborhood and of police demeanor toward members of minority groups. Somewhat over half of all Dominants thought that the police enjoyed a high reputation in the immediate neighborhood; only 3% said their reputation was low. Only 22% of the Negroes, however, and 31% of the Spanish-named thought the reputation of the police was high, while 7% of the Negroes and 9% of the Spanish-named thought it was low.

Minority members, and especially the Spanish-named, are much more critical of the job that police do in their own neighborhoods. Twenty-seven percent of the Dominants said that the police did an excellent job in their neighborhood; only 2% dissented. Among Negroes, 12% said police did an excellent job and 7% said they did a bad job. Among the Spanish-named, 11% said the job done was excellent and 13% said it was bad. As one can see, the unfavorable judgments of police performance were twice as common among Spanish-named as among Negroes, which in turn were three times as common as among Dominants.

The pervasive disenchantment of minorities with the police was clearly revealed in answers to questions dealing explicitly with police treatment of minorities. Almost three-fourths of all Dominants described police treatment as being always or usually fair. About half as many Negroes and Spanish-named agreed—42% of the Negroes and 45% of the Spanish-named. Only 4% of the Dominants thought treatment was often unfriendly or definitely prejudiced. On the other hand, 23% of the Negroes and 27% of the Spanish-named thought treatment was often unfriendly or definitely prejudiced. Besides the greater criticism of the police from minorities, two points should be noted. First, the amount of disagreement between Dominants and minorities on the issue of police treatment of minorities is substantial. Whatever the justice of minority complaints, the fact remains that Dominants perceive the situation very differently. They do not sympathize with the views of minorities. Second, almost half of the minority communities believe police treatment is always or usually fair. Thus, while criticism of police treatment is certainly more severe among minorities than Dominants, the evaluations of minorities are not inflexibly and uniformly negative. There is an appreciable amount of charitable judgments among minority people. This is a point that policemen and police reformers should keep in mind, for it indicates that there is a residuum of goodwill that might be utilized and built upon.

In the community as a whole there is a strong suspicion that who a person is affects how the police treat him. We have already seen[1] that the testimony of police officers lends credibility to this contention. The belief in inequality of treatment depending upon personal position is more than

[1] Chapter 4.

twice as common in the minority communities. Only 20% of Dominant respondents said that personal status affected treatment, while 56% of Negroes and 47% of Spanish-named said that it did. Urged to specify which kinds of people most commonly received different treatment, Dominants, Negroes, and Spanish-named all agreed that it was rich and influential people. Second and third in ranking came Negroes and Spanish-named, again regardless of the ethnicity of the respondent. The nature of the differing treatment is certainly radically different among these groups. Follow-up questions show that Denver citizens agree that the rich and powerful receive the best treatment, minority people the worst. Denver citizens agree among themselves that status does affect treatment of individuals and that inequality works against minorities and for the white, rich, and powerful.

The judgments that people make about the police, having to do with respect, reputation, quality of work performed, treatment of minorities, and differential behavior, are not affected by the age, sex, and social class of the respondent. Analysis fails to reveal any significant associations for any ethnic group between evaluative judgments and background variables. We conclude, therefore, that the most important factor influencing people's views of the police is ethnicity. Negroes and Spanish-named persons share among themselves views of the police that are less favorable than those of the rest of the community and which are not materially affected by the success they achieve in life in terms of social and economic position.

Our survey produced some evidence that minority people may also be more disenchanted with other segments of the criminal justice system than are Dominants. Sixty-four percent of Negroes and Spanish-named thought that people with money were more likely to be given a better break by judges when deciding cases in court. Only 39% of the Dominants agreed. Police officers were asked the same question, and their perceptions tallied with those of the Dominant majority. Minority people may very well be alienated from the entire system of legal adjudication. Their criticism of the police may not be unique in its unfavorableness. Study of minority problems might profitably focus on the particular grievances minority people have toward the courts and examine the expectations they take into contacts with the courts.

MINORITY EXPERIENCE WITH THE POLICE

Analysis of the survey data shows that ethnicity is a primary determinant of the amount and kind of contact people have with the police. Within ethnic groups there is by and large no association between age, sex, and class and whether an individual has been stopped and arrested or has called the police for help or talked over difficulties with them. In other words, the social background of the individual does not affect the proportion of contacts made with the police, regardless whether initiative in the contact is held by the private citizen or the police. There is one interesting exception to this. Analysis does show that education levels of Negroes and Spanish-named are associated with different rates of having been stopped and arrested by the police. However, contrary to what one might expect, the incidence of being stopped and arrested does not decline as educational attainments increase, especially for Negroes. To illustrate, from our intensive survey of 200 minority people,[2] 82% of Negroes who had finished eighth grade claimed that they had been stopped and arrested. For Negroes with some amount of high school, about 50% said they had been stopped and arrested. However, 75% of those Negroes who had one or two years of college said they had been stopped and arrested. In short, college-educated Negroes are almost as likely to have been arrested as Negroes with only an eighth-grade education. Sixty-eight percent of Spanish-named persons with an eighth-grade education reported having been arrested. The proportion fell among those with one, two, or three years of high school, but it rose once again to 65% of Spanish-named people who completed high school. Moreover, 50% of the Spanish-named who had one year of college said they had been stopped and arrested. So with the Spanish-named, too, education is not a protection against arrest. One concludes, therefore, that education, income, and occupation do not affect the likelihood of a minority person being arrested by the police.

The proportion of minority members who have called the police for help is the same as for Dominants—about 23%. The number of minority people who have discussed a problem with the police is less than for Dominants—13% for

[2] The nature of the four different surveys from which data was obtained for this study is explained in the Preface. The "intensive minority survey" involved in-depth interviews of exclusively minority group individuals. The "general public survey," from which most of the data used in this study was obtained, tapped opinions among all classes and ethnic groups in the city at large. The socioeconomic characteristics of the minority samples in both surveys were identical. The only survey difference between the minority samples involved the length of time taken by the interviews.

Dominants, 6% for Negroes, and 3% for Spanish-named. Moreover, among all governmental agencies the police are more important in terms of voluntary contacts for Dominants than for Negroes or the Spanish-named. The police force is the most contacted agency for Dominants; it is not for minority people. Thus, the conclusion is that, relative to their needs for law enforcement and their involvement with the police, measured in terms of proportion of arrests, minortiy people are considerably more reluctant to have contact with the police than are Dominants.[3]

The amount of firsthand contact by minority people with the police is substantial. About 45% of Negroes and the Spanish-named have either discussed a problem with the police or called the police for help at some time in their lives. Twenty-five percent did so in the past year.[4] In short, almost half of all minority people in Denver have had personally significant contacts with the police and half of these contacts have been recent. Thus, when minority people speak about the police they do so with considerable personal authority.

Informal contacts by the public with police vary only slightly among ethnic groups. About a third of all respondents acknowledge having a personal friend or acquaintance

[3] See the discussion of this point in Chapter 3.

[4] The intensive survey of minority groups showed that 54% of Negroes and 51% of the Spanish-named had been stopped and arrested at some time or other. It is very probable, therefore, that the figures from the general public survey underestimate the total amount of serious contact between police and minorities. Due to an oversight, a question was not included in the general public survey designed to determine the number of people who had been stopped and arrested. The intensive minority survey thus provides original data. The question is whether one can properly generalize from it to the general Negro and Spanish-named population. We think that one can.

on the police force. One out of every four people, again regardless of community, think that someone on the force has done a personal favor for them. The one item of difference among ethnic groups involved having had a friendly talk with policemen. Almost half of all Negroes and Dominants had had a friendly talk, but only a third of the Spanish-named had done so.

The experiences that members of minority groups had with the police are reported as being much less satisfactory than those of the majority community. Whereas almost half of the Dominants said they were satisfied with what the police did for them when called upon for help, only about a third of the Negroes and Spanish-named said the same.[5] The questions dealing with personal treatment meted out by the police revealed even more sharply the extent of minority group alienation. Ten percent of the Negroes and 24% of the Spanish-named said they or someone in their family had been badly treated by a police officer. Only 4% of the Dominants said this. The responses of Negroes were more like those of the Dominants than those of the Spanish-named. The data from this question are somewhat anomalous, for in the other personal-experience questions Negroes showed at least as many unpleasant experiences as had Spanish-named persons.

Negroes and Spanish-named persons have more personal experiences than Dominants that lead them to conclude that the police treat minority persons unfairly. Only 9% of the Dominants said they had a personal experience from which they conclude that the police do not treat all people equally. This is to be compared with 25% of the Negroes and 26% of the Spanish-named who cited a similar experience. Evi-

[5] Respectively, 47%, 34%, and 31%.

dence from the intensive minority survey indicates that the full measure of unfavorable minority experience with the police may not have been revealed in the general public survey. In the lengthy interviews of this survey 24% of the Negroes and 29% of the Spanish-named said they had had a personal experience which made them think the police did not treat all people alike.[6] A similar discrepancy between the two surveys was found in answers to another question. Respondents were asked whether they had ever seen a Negro or Spanish-named person being badly treated by the police. In the general public survey only 4% of the Dominants said they had, compared with 21% of the Negroes and 25% of the Spanish-named. In the intensive minority survey, using an identically worded question, 36% of the Negroes and 40% of the Spanish-named said they had seen a minority person badly treated by the police. Although there are several plausible explanations for the different responses between the two surveys, we do not have sufficient data to decide between them. The prudent course of interpretation is to utilize the more conservative data from the general public survey, recognizing, however, that it may seriously underestimate the amount of unfavorable personal experiences that minority people have had. Even utilizing the more conservative data, it is clear that minority people believe they have had personal experiences with police mistreatment of minorities in much larger proportions than Dominants.

This finding may be interpreted in several ways. It may

[6] *Task Force Report: The Police,* p. 147, noted that in-depth interviews were much more successful than ordinary surveys in getting at minority feelings about the police. They found that as interviews progressed neutral or favorable statements about the police became more hostile in tone. Our own experience supports this finding.

simply mean that Dominants are not generally familiar with minority life. Dominants are not in a position to have observed mistreatment of minority people. Or the data may indicate that minority people are more sensitive to police treatment and more ready to view it critically. They and the Dominants have seen the same events, but minority witnesses evaluate police behavior less favorably. Or, finally, majority and minority people may be viewing the situation quite objectively, their testimony revealing the presence of a real double standard in police operations. Whatever the explanation for this finding is, minority people are convinced they can cite personal evidence upon which to base grievances against the police. Data from another question support this conclusion. Among individuals who thought the police treated people differently depending on who they are, almost three times as many Negroes and Spanish-named as Dominants cited their own experience as the source of opinion. The lesson is that it will take actions and not just words to regenerate relations between police and minorities. There may well be inherited antipolice attitudes among Negroes and the Spanish-named, but the fact remains that these attitudes are being refueled constantly by personal experience. A change in police behavior will not create better relations overnight, if it can do so at all, but it is undoubtedly the basis for the reconstruction of opinion in minority communities.

Analysis of the survey data has shown that the quality of minority evaluations of the police are associated with the presence or absence of firsthand contact with the police. We concluded that the sheer fact of contact with the police, whether initiative is possessed by citizen or police, does influence opinions about the police. This being the case it is reasonable to expect that the character of contact with the police, especially if it is unpleasant, will have an even more profound effect on the attitudes people hold about the police. Analysis shows that this is true: there is an association between unpleasant personal experiences with the police and negative evaluations of them. Whatever the evaluation of the police may be, among all ethnic groups, people who have had some personal experience of an unpleasant kind with the police hold less favorable opinions than people who have not had these experiences. People who have been badly treated by police or have seen what they consider to be improper treatment will rate the police very critically indeed, whether they are talking about how police treat minorities, whether the city needs a civilian review board, whether the cause of riots is due to police brutality, whether different kinds of people are treated differently, and whether charges of brutality are by and large true. The lesson here is as old as the hills: good actions are outweighed by bad actions. A single instance of impropriety or mistreatment by a police officer may undo the patient work of multitudes of other officers.

Our data have shown that minority people carry into contacts with the police more negative expectations than do Dominants. One important result of these attitudes is the generation of a strong disposition to avoid the police. The operation of this disposition has already been shown by the figures on the amount of voluntary contacts minorities have relative to Dominants and relative to their own needs. Respondents were also asked directly whether they thought helping the police or cooperating with them was "just asking for a lot of trouble." Only 5% of the Dominants said this was true. On the other hand, 21% of the Negroes and

22% of the Spanish-named agreed with the statement. Results were almost identical in the intensive minority survey; this was not an occasion on which the two surveys differed. The intensive minority people were also given a follow-up question. They were asked to select from a group of statements those they would want their children to learn. Fifty-nine percent of the Negroes and 43% of the Spanish-named selected the statement "Don't get involved with the police."

The policeman that the minority person makes contact with is almost always a member of the majority community. Only twenty-two officers,[7] amounting to 2.7% of the force, are Negroes or Spanish-named. The ethnicity of the officer does make a difference with some people—especially among Dominants and the Spanish-named. Four out of five respondents in every community said they did not care what the ethnicity of the officer was whom they went to for help or advice. Among the remaining 20%—those who did prefer to deal with an officer of a particular ethnicity—Dominants and the Spanish-named preferred to deal with someone in their own community. Twelve percent of the Dominants and 10% of the Spanish-named admitted they would prefer to deal with someone from their own community. Eight percent of the Negroes said they would rather deal with a Negro and another 8% said they would rather deal with a Dominant officer. Not one Negro said he would prefer to deal with a Spanish-named officer, though 2% of the Spanish-named said they would prefer to deal with a Negro. The pattern of sociable contacts with policemen supports the presumption that ethnicity is an important factor. Of the people with personal acquaintances among policemen of their neighborhood, not a single Dominant respondent had

[7] Early 1968.

either a Negro or Spanish-named friend. Among Negroes, some had Negro friends and some Dominant friends, but none had a Spanish-named friend. Spanish-named people had Dominant or Spanish-named friends on the force, but none of them had a Negro friend. The world of liking and disliking is not divided into two halves; it has divisions among minority groups that must be considered by people responsible for recruiting and deploying policemen.

There do not seem to be strong negative reactions among minority people to minority policemen. Only 8% of the Negroes and 5% of the Spanish-named said they thought of such officers as traitors or did not respect them. Over 70% of all minority people said they thought they were doing a good job, respected them, and thought they were helping the cause.

POLICE BRUTALITY

The most dramatic charge that can be made against the police in their relations with the public is that of brutality. Most of the urban riots in recent years have had an alleged incident of police brutality as the pretext. Certainly charges of police brutality are not uncommon; they are reported almost daily in newspapers and on radio and television. While most people are aware of the issue, it is much more important to minorities. Forty-six percent of the majority population said they had heard charges of police brutality. Among Negroes 68% said they had heard such charges, and among the Spanish-named, 59%. Most people, regardless of community, got their information through the news media. However, the proportion of people in the minority communities who heard the charges from friends or neighbors was much greater than among Dominants. Where only 4% of the Dominants obtained their information from friends and neighbors, 30% of the Negroes and 12% of the Spanish-named had done so. Moreover, whereas only 4% of the Dominants had personal experience with police brutality, 9% of the Negroes and 15% of the Spanish-named had. There can be no doubt that minority communities are much more attuned to the issue than the majority community.

The police are aware of the charge too, indeed more than anyone else. Like the public, the mass media are their best source of information—22% cited this source. The next more important source was fellow police officers, who correspond to the "friends and neighbors" of the minority people. For policemen, like minority people, "police brutality" is an issue which is in the air they breathe; it is the stuff of daily conversation among their peers. Officers cited as their next most important sources of information about charges of police brutality, minority people, suspects, and arrested persons.

Before one can really deal with the issue, it is important to be clear about what "police brutality" is. It is not a straightforward category. Holding a suspect and beating him with a rubber hose would certainly be brutality. But is arm-twisting in order to get a person to enter a patrol car? Are threats, such as gestures with gun or nightstick, brutality? Bayard Rustin once said: "I don't know a Negro family that has not had a member who has not met with physical or spiritual brutality on the part of the police."[8] If brutality

[8] Thomas R. Brooks, "Necessary Force—Or Police Brutality?" *New York Times Magazine,* December 5, 1965, 65.

is synonymous with mistreatment of any kind, then verbal abuse, ridicule, malicious humor, denigrating epithets, and elaborate condescension would all qualify. People can certainly be hurt as deeply by being dismissed with contempt as by being struck or manhandled. In order to cope with the difficulty of defining police brutality, we asked respondents what they meant by it. As one would expect, the vast majority thought of the use of physical force, the doing of bodily harm. Most revealing, however, were the answers from minority people. Thirteen percent of the Negroes and 15% of the Spanish-named listed as police brutality not listening to the other side of the story, taking situations into their hands without consideration for the people involved, unfair use of authority and misuse of law. Furthermore, 3% of the Negroes and 5% of the Spanish-named cited unfriendliness, suspicion, and prejudice. Only 4% of the Dominants thought of these other activities as constituting police brutality. In fact, among Dominants the second most popular response (14%) was to deny that police brutality existed or to argue that force was necessary or that the charge was trumped up by criminals. Another 8% of the Dominants argued that, though physical mistreatment was what they meant by police brutality, it was for the most part provoked by the people dealt with by the police. In other words, Dominant citizens can hardly imagine brutality in any form other than physical violence, and many of them believe the whole issue is overdone. The gap between minority and majority perspectives revealed by these responses should give pause to even the most optimistic reformer of majority-minority relations.

One is justified in concluding that when people hear the phrase "police brutality," they have in mind by-and-large physical assaults. This is the meaning that will be adopted in the following discussion.

It should also be noted that police brutality is not just a descriptive category. Rather, it is a judgment made about the propriety of police behavior. Not all examples of the use of physical force by policemen are instances of brutality. The phrase connotes that what the police have done is unjustified, not required by circumstances. Since the use of the phrase implies a judgment, people may disagree profoundly about whether a particular incident, even though it involves the obvious use of force, is a case of brutality. Any discussion of police brutality is therefore encumbered by confusion about whether it applies to more than physical assaults and also by disagreement over what circumstances absolve the police from blame. Just as the content of police brutality is a function of perspective, and in turn, a consequence of social position in the community, so judgments about the circumstances that exculpate the police are also a function of perspective. The phrase "police brutality" must be used with great care, and people should not be at all surprised to discover that minority groups weigh it much differently than does the majority community.

The willingness to believe charges of police brutality leveled by minority individuals varies dramatically among ethnic groups. Only 8% of the Dominants said they were prepared to believe the frequent charges. Among Negroes, on the other hand, 37% said the charges were true, and among Spanish-named, 39%. The police were even more skeptical of minority charges than was the Dominant community as a whole: 88% of the officers said that less than 5% of the charges were true. Whatever the amount of truth actually in the charges, the fact remains that a world of difference separates the perspectives of the minority and majority communities on this issue. Minority people are prone to believe; majority people are prone to discount. The result is that majority people dismiss minority claims as exaggerated; minority people conclude they cannot get a sympathetic hearing from the majority community.

Analysis shows no evidence that class affects whether a person has heard charges of brutality or his willingness to accept them as true. Ethnicity, not class, is the deciding variable. We do find, however, that Negro and Spanish-named men are more apt to have heard of police brutality than women. This may simply mean they are more sensitive to the issue than women.

Over twice as many Negroes as Dominants and over twice as many Spanish-named as Negroes claimed that they or someone in their family had been badly treated by the Denver police. The proportions were 4% for Dominants, 10% for Negroes, and 24% for the Spanish-named. The nature of the bad treatment varied according to ethnic group. Physical brutality in some form was more prominent among Negroes and Spanish-named. Sixty-one percent of the Negroes and 63% of the Spanish-named who had been badly treated gave this as their reason; only 26% of the Dominants said physical brutality was the problem. Moreover, whereas 36% of the Dominants thought that their bad treatment was a matter of the police being unfair or unwarranted in their action, only 22% of the Negroes and 21% of the Spanish-named gave this as their reason. Thus, minority individuals experience a higher incidence of what they consider to be bad treatment and the forms this treatment assumes are more serious than those experienced by Dominants. Physical abuse is more commonly experienced by minorities.

Analysis reveals no important associations between having experienced bad treatment and social background. Class is unrelated to the incidence of bad treatment. This finding gives credence to the charge of well-to-do Negroes with professional status that they are subjected to the same kind of humiliations that all Negroes experience. Professional attainments do not hide the color of their skins. Young Negro men (teen-agers and twenty-one to thirty years old) have a higher incidence of being badly treated than older people. This may indicate that they are in fact singled out for harassment more often than others or that they have a much greater sensitivity to the slights of police contact.[9] Whichever the explanation, young Negroes have had experiences with the police that do not dispose them favorably toward policemen.

It should be noted that the vast majority of minority people have *not* been badly treated by the police. This does not excuse the bad treatment which has been meted out, but it does put into perspective the magnitude of the problem. Responses from the intensive survey of minorities reveal a more somber picture. Among the minority members who had contact with the police, 60% of the Negroes and 45% of the Spanish-named said the treatment was all right. Another 8% of the Negroes and 7% of the Spanish-named said it was all right but cold and distant. Twenty-seven percent

[9] Teen-age Negroes have complained about being harassed by the police. They complained especially about being treated as eternal objects of suspicion, frequently being stopped for questioning or treated curtly, authoritatively, or rudely. See *The Denver Post*, August 22, 1967, p. 2.

of the Negroes and 36.8% of the Spanish-named said they had been treated with disrespect, cursed, manhandled, or roughed up. Thus, while most minority people cannot complain about discriminatory police treatment at first hand, many of them can—and the proportion is far larger than among Dominants. These facts are hardly a matter for congratulation of policemen.

When unfair police treatement of minorities is being discussed, what seems to be troubling minority people most is not the outright use of an unwarranted amount of force. Rather, they are more concerned about harassment in the form of street interrogations and arrests on spurious grounds. For example, in the intensive minority survey, when respondents were asked to specify the ways in which police made life more difficult for Negroes and the Spanish-named, the most common complaint was that of harassment (21% of Negroes and 26% of Spanish-named). Outright brutality was fourth in the Negro list, accounting for 4% of the total, and fourth in the Spanish-named list, accounting for 4% of the total. In short, minorities are sensitive about their position; they know they are peculiarly visible. Policemen reinforce this feeling when they appear to single minority people out for special attention. Even if policemen were, therefore, to abandon any form of physical coercion directed at minority people, wariness of the police would continue to remain strong among minorities as long as the police appeared to be looking upon them with chronic suspicion.

Policemen proved to be surprisingly candid about their own personal experience with police brutality. Fifty-three percent of the officers sad that they had personally witnessed an incident that someone might consider to constitute police brutality. A third of these incidents the officers dismissed as involving the necessary, and justifiable, application of force, usually in connection with making an arrest. But it is significant that 27% of all officers interviewed had witnessed an incident which they considered involved harassment or the excessive use of force. Curiously enough, the proportion of personal experience with "brutality" is approximately the same among policemen as it is among minority people.

COMPLAINTS AGAINST THE POLICE

For all the suspicion shown by minority people toward the police and the unpleasant personal experiences they have had with them, very few have made formal complaints about police behavior. Ten percent of Negroes and 24% of the Spanish-named in our sample said they had been badly treated by the police; 9% of Negroes and 15% of the Spanish-named had personal experience with police brutality. Yet only 4% of the Negroes and 4% of the Spanish-named had actually made a complaint about the police to someone in authority. The rate of complaint among minorities is, however, higher than among Dominants: only 2% of the Dominants had made a complaint, as against 4% of them who had been badly treated and 4% of them who had had a personal experience with police brutality. The data does not show that relative to the incidence of complaint-worthy behavior minority people are more reluctant to complain than are Dominants. Minority people have more personal experience with mistreatment and they also complain more. By and large the proportion of complaints about misbehavior of the police either seen or experienced by each community is the same. One cannot conclude, therefore, that the unequal treatment of minorities has affected their willingness, relative to Dominants, to lodge complaints against the police. One might save this proposition by assuming that the seriousness of the provocations were greater in the case of Negroes and the Spanish-named than among Dominants. This may in fact be true.

The evidence very clearly shows that people, regardless of ethnicity, do not complain against the police automatically when they feel aggrieved. People commonly accept what is done to them without trying to buck the system. It might also be added that 2% as against 4% of the adult population, which is the proportion of adults that made a complaint, is not a small number of people. It amounts to about ten thousand people. Examining the figures more closely, we discover that, in the year immediately preceding the survey, 2% of the Dominants, Negroes, and Spanish-named respondents had made a complaint. If this figure is representative of other years, then about six thousand people a year lodge a complaint with higher authorities about the police. The rate would be about twenty-six per day. This is a sizable number of people, and their feelings of disenchantment as well as their reactions to the complaint process could be a powerful leaven in the loaf of police-community relations.

Analysis does not show any association between being willing to complain and background characteristics of respondents. One cannot conclude, for example, that people with higher incomes and more education are more likely to complain. Willingness to complain seems to be a function of what happens to people and what they expect to be able to gain from it, and these factors are not class-specific. We do find that people with more negative evaluations of the police are more apt to have made a complaint. This is what one would expect.

Of those people who had lodged a complaint, most were concerned about what they referred to as "police brutality" and "rudeness."[10]

Compared to people who made a complaint, a larger proportion had considered filing a complaint at some time or other about the police but had decided against following through. The proportions were 6% among Dominants, 12% among Negroes, and 15% among the Spanish-named. As with the figures on those actually having made complaints, the rate is about twice as high among minorities, a figure which is roughly proportional to the relative incidence of unequal treatment or mistreatment among minorities.[11] The most prevalent cause for potential complaints among Dominants were traffic or motor vehicle violations; this pretext was second in importance among minority people. With Negroes and the Spanish-named the most important cause was police brutality. Among Negroes police brutality out-polled the next most important pretext two to one; among the Spanish-named police brutality outpolled the next most important pretext three to one. Therefore, while the data show that minorities believe themselves to be much more afflicted by police brutality than Dominants, the majority community is not completely unfamiliar with it. Twenty-six percent of the Dominants who thought about complaining

---

[10] This was an open-ended question.

[11] It is worth noting that the intensive minority survey produced a larger proportion of potential complainants. Twenty-one percent of Negroes and 24% of the Spanish-named had considered making a complaint but decided against it. Once again, therefore, the data show that intensive interviews produce more critical information about police-minority relations.

but did not do so had as a pretext police brutality, compared to 34.8% among Negroes and 55% among the Spanish-named.

The reasons people gave for failing to follow through on a complaint reveal a lack of real concern with the problem or a conclusion on their part that complaining will not do any good. They either did not want to take the time or did not believe that anyone would listen sympathetically if they did. The proportion of potential complainers who indicated that complaning wouldn't do any good—that "no one would listen"—was 26.2% among Dominants, 20% among Negroes, and 45.5% among Spanish-named. It is clear that a lack of confidence in the responsiveness of the system is only part of the story explaining why more people did not complain. In a larger proportion of cases—except among the Spanish-named—people simply did not want to be bothered; the complaint was not as important as the time they would have had to devote to it.

Police and minority people share different ideas about what should be done with complaints about mistreatment at the hands of the police. Police officers overwhelmingly said that a complainant should contact the Internal Affairs Bureau of the police department. The Internal Affairs Bureau is formally charged with receiving and processing complaints. Police officers also indicated that they would advise a complainant to contact a superior officer or the Chief himself. Officers, not surprisingly, have faith that the police system will render justice to the complainant. Only 7% of them suggested that they would advise an aggrieved citizen to contact an attorney, the District Attorney's Office, or the Mayor. Minority persons, however, overwhelmingly indicated they would advise someone to appeal outside the police establishment. For example, of those minority individuals who specified a particular channel for complaints, 59.5% of the Negroes and 63.3% of the Spanish-named cited a nonpolice agency. Only 25% of the Negroes and 10% of the Spanish-named indicated a police authority. Among those recommending an appeal to the police establishment, most cited the Chief of Police; none of the Spanish-named and only 8% of the Negroes mentioned the Internal Affairs Bureau.

Our study shows that faith in the police establishment itself when it comes to vindicating mistreatment is not very great. The question then arises, would the creation of an independent complaint-receiving and investigating agency serve a useful purpose? Some cities have tried this, through the establishment of what is usually called a civilian review board. One could argue that if such an agency were created the volume of legitimate complaints made by aggrieved persons would rise, thus serving to provide essential information to public officials about police activities and for redress of grievance to the harassed citizen. The only way to test whether the volume of justified complaints would actually rise would be by establishing the review board. Our data has already shown that some people do not complain because they doubt that anyone will listen. However, a larger portion indicated they did not complain because they could not be bothered; the issue was not as important to them as the time involved in making the complaint. It is possible, of course, that one reason people cannot be bothered is because they have imperfect knowledge of how to make a complaint. Their lack of knowledge makes the process seem more formidable than it really is. As previously mentioned the formal mechanism for receiving complaints

within the police in Denver is the Internal Affairs Bureau.
The intensive survey of minority people disclosed that 22%
of Negroes and 10% of Spanish-named people had heard of
the unit. However, only 10% of Negroes and 2% of the
Spanish-named could correctly identify the Internal Affairs
Bureau as the unit that receives citizen complaints and
watches over police behavior. Because the Internal Affairs
Bureau is not widely known and because minority people
seem to lack faith in achieving satisfaction through the
police establishment itself, it seems that the creation of a
civilian review board probably would result in the registering of a larger number of complaints.

Even if the volume of complaints does not rise with
the creation of an independent complaint-receiving agency,
one can still argue that it would serve a useful purpose by
demonstrating that the police force is not a closed corporation, immune from examination. In this way a civilian
review board might help to restore public confidence in the
police, especially among minority persons, even though the
actual volume of legitimate complaints filed would not increase. Our study has shown that minority people in Denver
are indeed suspicious of the police to a much larger extent
than the majority population. Furthermore, they do tend to
look upon a civilian review board much more favorably
than Dominants. Whereas 47% of the Dominants were favorably disposed toward the creation of a civilian review board,
73% of Negroes and 71% of the Spanish-named were favorably disposed. Twenty-four percent of the Dominants were
opposed to the idea, while only 8% of the Negroes and 6%
of the Spanish-named were opposed to it. There is little
doubt that minority people do look upon the establishment
of an independent complaint-receiving agency as an im-

portant matter. Whether the creation of such a unit would produce a permanent rise in confidence in the police force remains an open question. But the indications are that it might.

Denver policemen very seriously underestimate the strength of sentiment among minorities, indeed among Dominants too, for the creation of a civilian review board. Only 11% of the Denver police officers believe that the general public wants it. Policemen are either very much out of touch with public opinion or they are projecting upon the public their own hostility to the idea. Eighty-nine percent of policemen believe that the creation of a civilian review board is a "bad idea." Only 4% of them support it. When asked why they disliked the idea, most officers indicated that civilians could not be expected to approach police problems with sufficient understanding. They would not know the frustrations, tensions, constraints, and ambiguities of police life. In effect, police officers are saying that there is a gap in understanding of the requirements of effective police action between police and public. If civilian members, not having learned about police work from the inside, were allowed to oversee what is being done, disciplinary actions would be undertaken that would hurt morale and, because policemen believe in the social value of what they do, would unfavorably affect public safety. The point to underscore is that *both* police and minorities believe that the nature of their relations with one another is not understood by outsiders. The minorities want to solve the problem through impartial publicity. The police doubt that outside observation can be impartial.

What is striking in the views of police officers is the implicit presumption that civilians cannot or will not understand and the consequent reluctance on the part of officers to work openly with them to develop a proper—and mutual —understanding of the problems and constraints of police work. No doubt police officers are right in viewing the attempt by minorities to establish civilian review boards as a threat to their independence; minorities certainly do want to restrain police activity of certain kinds. The issue of the civilian review board reveals clearly that police and minorities are locked in an adversary relationship. As was shown so dramatically in the struggle over a civilian review board in New York City, a gain for one side is considered a defeat for the other. This is unfortunate, particularly when the primary objective of a review board is to obtain impartial information about the nature of the relationship. In lieu of the findings of an independent agency, the community will have to make do with the charges and countercharges of combatants.

The President's Commission on Law Enforcement and Criminal Justice, while strongly recommending that complaint procedures within police forces needed to be simple, effective, and well publicized, argued against establishment of civilian review boards.[12] Their contention was that there is no reason to single out the police for special treatment. There should be effective channels for registering and investigating complaints against any government servant, whatever the department he belongs to. That the problem of adequate complaint machinery extends beyond the police force is demonstrated in our survey. Forty-eight percent of the Dominants, 37% of the Negroes, and 54% of the Spanish-named said they had no idea what bureau, agency, or de-

[12] *The Challenge of Crime in a Free Society,* p. 103. An extended discussion is presented in *Task Force Report: The Police,* pp. 198-205.

partment to go to if subjected to improper treatment by a municipal agency. The Commission's point seems to have been that it is not the principle of civilian review that is bad, but rather that the problem is government-wide and hence the solution should be equally extensive. Hidden behind the Commission's recommendation may have been a tactical consideration: policemen may be less likely to oppose civilian review if it does not seem to imply criticism of them particularly. The ambitious solution the Commission proposes is correct and admirable; what the Commission overlooks however is that once the issue of a civilian review board for the police is joined, its handling by government can critically affect police-community relations. If police-minority relations are fragile, communities should be advised that it may be unwise to postpone too long a good solution for the sake of a better one.

POLICE IN THE MINORITY WORLD

The study has shown that minority people are, compared to Dominants, more critical of the police, much more willing to see racial slights in police actions, more suspicious of police activities, and more subject to mistreatment, harassment, and brutality. In all these features of relation with the police, ethnicity and not social class are correlative. People within ethnic groups share much more in common with respect to relations with the police than do people of similar class. Minority people look for assistance from the police in much the same kinds of situations majority persons do, with two exceptions. Minority people, probably because their level of income is lower, are less involved with motor vehicle problems. Furthermore, minority people utilize the police in nonenforcement emergencies, particularly sickness, much more than do majority people.

Minority people are not unaware of the uncertain stance which members of their group take up against the police. Minority people in the survey were asked to specify ways in which Negroes and the Spanish-named made the work of the police more difficult. One-third of the respondents denied that minority people *did* make police work more difficult. However, 38% of the Negroes and 28% of the Spanish-named said that minority people were uncooperative, resentful, and likely to rebel against the police. Another 11% of Negroes and 13% of Spanish-named recognized that minority people had a higher rate of criminal infractions.

It is clear that minority people are sensitive to the quality of their relations with the police. They are convinced their ethnic status tells against them, and if they have not made up their minds that the police are uniformly prejudiced, they are alert for any sign that the latter might be. Conceding, then, that the police are a problem for minority people, the question arises as to how important this problem is among the many difficulties associated with minority status? How seminal are the police in the minority world? How important for minorities would it be to achieve better police relations? To what extent would an improvement in police relations lighten the burdens of minority life?

When asked to comment on the features of life in Denver that were the hardest to bear, minority people cited most frequently the general problem of discrimination and prejudice and the difficulty in gaining adequate employment. Among the many problems Negroes mentioned, the police ranked fourth. For the Spanish-named the police were among several problems, such as housing, that ranked sixth in the list of primary difficulties. Only 6% of the Negroes and 4% of the Spanish-named listed police as the unfavorable feature of life in Denver that they thought of first. Similar answers were obtained when people were asked what particular problems they thought poor people in Denver had most difficulty with. Dominants, Negroes, and the Spanish-named all agreed that making ends meet was the primary problem. Next came, in an order that depended upon the ethnic group, employment, housing, and education. Police brutality and harassment ranked eighth among Negroes (5%) and the Spanish-named (8%). Only 2% of the Dominants mentioned it. In the intensive interviews with minority people, 1% of the Negroes and 3% of the Spanish-named cited police as the source of a particular gripe or complaint they wanted to make about life in Denver.

The public was asked to specify the one thing more than any other they would like to see changed for the better in their immediate neighborhood. Improvement in police protection and law enforcement, including traffic and parking offenses, was cited by 4% of the Negroes and 5% of the Spanish-named. Seven percent of the Dominants made the same recommendation. A larger proportion of minority people were concerned about physical improvements, such as better street lighting, storm sewers, and cross-walks, or housing repairs, and a greater number of parks and recreational facilities than were concerned about the police. Even in the intensive minority interviews, when more candid and unfavorable opinions about the police were elicited, the preoccupation was with physical improvements, more adequate housing, and improved recreational facilities. Three percent of the Negroes and 2% of the Spanish-named cited better law enforcement and traffic controls.

Among the many afflictions of minority people, police protection and police treatment are not especially salient problems. That is, there are a host of other things that minority people feel ought to be done first in order to make an improvement in their lives. One can hardly conclude, on the basis of this testimony, that amelioration of police-community relations will get at the heart of minority discontents. At the same time, it is also clear from the survey that police are an especially visible part of the minority world. Police were mentioned along with the Denver Welfare Department, Colorado Employment Service, and Denver General Hospital as the agencies that gave minority groups trouble. Complaints about the police seem to be common throughout the community. Among Dominants, in fact, it tops the list of agencies people had heard complaints about; among Negroes the police rank second (by one percentage point) and among the Spanish-named third. Twenty-one percent of Negroes cited the police as the agency they had heard complaints about, compared to 11% among Dominants and 8% among the Spanish-named. The Denver Welfare Department was most frequently cited as the object of complaint by both Negroes and the Spanish-named.

The relative sensitivity of the police as an issue among the major ethnic groups was shown in the answers to a question about what was the primary cause of riots and violence among minority people. Both Negroes and the Spanish-named mentioned discrimination and unequal treatment generally as the primary cause (36% and 29% respectively). Next in importance for Negroes was police brutality and harassment (18%); this cause was fifth in importance among the Spanish-named (12%). Dominants, on the other hand, said that the primary cause was outside agitators, Communists, and troublemakers (35%). The *least* important reason in their view was police brutality and harassment. The testimony of these groups reveals an astonishing difference in perceptions about the reality and effects of police activity in the life of the minority community. With respect to the police, minority and majority people live in completely different worlds.

The police are important for minority people not just because of what they do but because of what they are. Minority people recognize that other problems must be solved if substantial improvements are to be made in the quality of their lives. Yet what they experience at the hands of the police is of enormous emotional significance. It symbolizes for them the backhanded treatment they receive from society as a whole. The police are the ubiquitous, public, authority-laden symbols of their own second-class citizenship. Upon them is vented the accumulated frustrations of lifetimes of inequality and subservience. As one commentator has trenchantly put it: "The policeman is a 'Rorschach' in uniform as he patrols his beat."[13] Minority people project upon him their emotional reactions to deprivation at the hands of the majority.

In sum, the position the police occupy in the minority world is only partly a result of what police do in that world; more importantly, their position is a function of fundamental emotional judgments made by people subjected to pervasive deprivation and inequality. This being the case, substantial improvements in police-minority relations cannot be expected solely as the result of changes in police policy and behavior. It will be necessary to change their symbolic status as well, and that is a function of a total

[13] Niederhoffer, *op. cit.,* p. 1.

system of majority-minority relationships. Reform in certain police practices must certainly be undertaken. There are ways in which the police may lessen the hostility they attract. However, in order to make a dent in deeply ingrained habits of mind among minority people, passed on as part of the legacy of minority status, the changes must be thorough, visible, and permanent. One cannot realistically expect an instantaneous regeneration of police-minority relations. Improvement will take years, possibly generations. At the same time, those who would ameliorate the relations between police and minorities must also realize that it may not be within the power of the police to do much more than palliate the situation, no matter how heroic their efforts to change. In order to produce better police-community relations changes in police behavior and practice must be one part of a program touching all those aspects of human interaction which create minority status. For the police will continue to function as a lightning rod for minority discontent so long as they must enforce laws created by a community with which minority people only imperfectly identify.

A change in police behavior, then, necessary though it is, cannot be expected to eliminate the corroding distrust and massive unrest evident today in the minority communities. Police reform is not a substitute for social reform. Moreover, changes in police behavior may not even be able to produce a great deal of improvement in police-minority relations unless it is coupled with a program of social renovation so penetrating and effective that it shatters the barriers which make majority and minority communities coherent social groups.

6

The Police
Confront
Minorities

Having seen in the previous chapter how the police appear to members of minority groups, we shall now put on
police eyeglasses to see how minorities appear to policemen.
It will be necessary to examine the emotional predispositions of policemen toward minority people, their understanding of minority problems, and their ability to empathize
with minority demands. The treatment which policemen
have received at the hands of minorities and what policemen expect from them will also be determined. In this way
one can begin to understand how policemen feel constrained
to act toward minority persons.

ARE POLICEMEN PREJUDICED?

Are policemen prejudiced? The answer is yes, but only slightly more so than the community as a whole. Policemen reflect the dominant attitudes of the majority people towards minorities. Consequently, if one thinks it is fair to characterize our society as prejudiced—a view we adopt—then the data show that the police are prejudiced.

For example, police officers and members of the public were asked to state whether they liked or disliked Negroes, Jews, and the Spanish-named. An index of the responses was constructed running from zero to six, with higher scores indicating greater dislike. The average score for policemen was 1.75, and for the Dominant public 0.84. A larger portion of police officers had higher rankings than the Dominant public. To illustrate, 48% of the officers had scores of three or higher; only 14% of the public scored as high. Thirty-seven percent of the police had zero scores, indicating no dislike whatsoever of minority groups, while 60% of the general public scored as low. The median score for police and general public was two.

Eight percent of police officers said they disliked the Spanish-named, compared to 5.6% of the Dominant public; 5% of the officers disliked Negroes, compared with 5.05% of the public; and 2% of the officers disliked Jews, compared with 1.8% of the public (see Table 6-1). It should be noted that a majority of policemen and the Dominant public said they *liked* these minorities. It is only a minority that is willing to admit to prejudice.

Police and the general public were also presented with specific situations of personal interaction and asked if the presence of a Negro, Jew, or Spanish-named individual would upset them. Four forms of personal interrelation were presented: eating together at the same table, participating in a party involving predominantly minority people, dancing with a partner from a minority group, and having someone in the immediate family marry a minority person. An index indicating intensity of the upset reaction was constructed for each minority group, running from zero to four.

TABLE 6–1

WHETHER OR NOT MAJORITY MEMBERS OF THE DENVER POLICE DEPARTMENT AND THE DOMINANT PUBLIC WOULD SAY ON THE WHOLE THAT THEY LIKE OR DISLIKE MEMBERS OF MINORITY GROUPS

Minority Groups	Denver Police			Dominant Public		
	Like %	Dislike %	Total %	Like %	Dislike %	Total %
Spanish-named	51	8	59*	62	6	68†
Jewish	62	2	64*	71	2	73†
Negroes	53	5	58*	61	5	66†

* Thirty-two Denver police said either "don't care" or "neither" to above question on Spanish-named, and four said question "doesn't apply"; twenty-six policemen in answer to question on Jews said either "don't care" or "neither" and four said question "doesn't apply"; thirty-three policemen in answer to question on Negroes said "neither" or "don't care" and four said question "doesn't apply."

† For Spanish-named: 78, or 23%, of the Dominant public (majority group) said "neither" or "don't care"; 12, or 4%, said "don't know"; 19, or 6%, said question didn't apply; and 1 person did not respond. For Jewish: 62, or 18%, said "neither" or "don't care"; 8, or 2%, said they didn't know; 20, or 6%, said question did not apply; and 1 person did not respond. For Negroes: 83, or 25%, said "neither" or "don't care"; 9, or 3%, said they didn't know; 20, or 6%, said question did not apply; and 2, or 1%, did not respond.

Police officers were slightly less prejudiced against Jews than the Dominant public (0.5 vs. 0.89), slightly less prejudiced against the Spanish-named than the Dominant public (0.71 vs. 0.99), and slightly more prejudiced against Negroes than the Dominant public (1.8 vs. 1.68).

Among officers and the Dominant public, prejudice is least evident against Jews, most against Negroes, with Spanish-named people occupying an intermediate position, although closer to Jews than Negroes in intensity of dislike shown them. For example, the Dominant public's composite upset score for Negroes was 1.68, for the Spanish-named 0.99, and for Jews 0.89. On the like-dislike scale, in contrast to the prejudice scale, the Dominant public put the Spanish-named much closer to the Negroes. In fact there is little to distinguish them on this scale from Negroes.

As one would expect, revulsion against mixing is strongest with respect to marriage and least strong with respect to eating together at the same table. Less than 1% of the policemen and less than 5% of the Dominant public said they would be upset if they had to share a table at meal times with a member of a minority group. A much greater amount of antipathy was shown about going to a party and finding that most of the people there were members of a minority group. Thirty-six percent of the police and 34% of the public said they would be upset if the minority people involved were Negroes; 16% and 17% respectively if Spanish-named people were involved; and 4% and 8% if Jews were involved. Curiously, although policemen and public indicated they would be as upset about dancing with a minority person as going to a party dominated by them if the people involved were Negro, both officers and public were less offended by dancing with Jews and the Spanish-named than going to a party dominated by them. None of the policemen and 5% of the Dominant public said they would be upset to dance with a Jew, compared to 4% of the officers and 8% of the public who would be upset by going to a party dominated by Jews. Similarly, 2% of the officers and 13% of the public would be upset by dancing with a Spanish-named person, but 16% of the officers and

17% of the Dominant public would be upset by going to a party dominated by the Spanish-named. It would seem that, with respect to Jews and the Spanish-named, majority people are not affronted by physical contact as such but rather by being surrounded and outnumbered by them. With Jews and the Spanish-named there is a sense of distance and alienation, but physical contact is not in itself contaminating. Thus they would be willing to dance with them but still feel uncomfortable having to mix with them socially. With Negroes, however, majority people feel both social distance and the contaminating effects of physical contact.

The highest upset scores were registered in connection with marriage within the immediate family to a member of a minority group. Eighty-five percent of the police officers and 84% of the public said they would be upset if the marriage was with a Negro. Less than half as many, 33% of the officers and 44% of the public would be upset if the partner were Spanish-named. And 14% of the officers and 25% of the public would be upset if the marriage was with a Jew.

In sum, police officers share the ethnic prejudices of the community as a whole. Within Denver, Negroes are farthest from the pale. Moreover, the quality of the gap between Negro and Dominants seems less bridgeable and more emotionally involved than the gap between the majority community and any other ethnic group. Between Negroes and Dominants there is not only the sense of difference, but a strong suggestion that contact itself is somehow contaminating. The chances of healing the breach between Negroes and Dominants and producing a genuinely integrated society would seem to be considerably less than with Jews and the Spanish-named.

POLICE SYMPATHY FOR MINORITY PROBLEMS

Very little credence is given by policemen to charges that policemen treat minority people unfairly or improperly. About a quarter of all officers do believe that police treatment varies, depending upon the kind of person contacted. And 6% of the officers believe that minority people attract different behavior. Asked specifically to characterize the demeanor of policemen in dealing with minority people, 5% said that policemen were sometimes unfriendly. No officer said they were prejudiced or antagonistic. A small minority of officers are willing to say that policemen sometimes do treat minority people in an unfriendly way—which must be true for almost any group the police contact—but that this is not a product of fundamental attitudes.

One could argue that these responses cannot be taken at face value. They do not indicate that policemen do not believe the charges leveled against the police, but rather that police officers will not admit such charges to be correct. A police organization is a closed corporation; access is gained on a "need to know" basis. Policemen are conscious of having to defend the organization against the slurs of detractors; they are loath to give ammunition to outsiders. They also recognize that partiality toward minority groups is the gravest sin an officer can commit. For all these reasons, one can argue that whatever officers say about the truth of these charges is bound to understate their true opinions. At the same time, police officers may have been perfectly candid. The interviews for the survey were strictly private, conducted in each officer's home; the pledge of secrecy about attributing opinions to individuals was accepted without question, perhaps because the reputation of a university stood behind it; and the cooperation obtained from officers was outstanding. Therefore, while there may have been distortion in the police responses, the direction of it remains for us an open question.

Very few officers believe the many charges of police brutality leveled by minority groups. In fact nine out of ten officers said that less than 5% of the charges were true. Their disinclination to believe is as much a function of the large number of charges made as to a finding on the police officer's part that brutality never takes place. A quarter of all the officers interviewed said they had witnessed an incident involving harassment or the excessive use of force. Officers are saying, in effect, that brutality may occur from time to time, and it may be unjustified by circumstances, but that most people who cry "brutality" are mistaken.

Policemen are not entirely sure among themselves what kind of punishment should be meted out to the officer who is proven to be hostile and antagonistic toward minorities. Two out of five believe that such an officer should be dismissed from the force. The rest believe that he should remain on the force but be disciplined, transferred, or educated. Thirty-four percent, for example, say he should be taken off his present job or moved to a noncontact post, though not dismissed. Policemen realize that a prejudiced policeman is a serious problem for them, but they do not seem to believe that he cannot still perform some useful service for the department.

Only a minority of policemen believe that their reputation for impartiality is so low that minority people hesitate to contact the police. Thirty-one percent said this was the case; 63% denied it. Since evidence has already been presented supporting the proposition that minority people do hesitate to call the police in greater measure than Dominants, one concludes that policemen are out of touch with the true sentiments of minority people.

Denver policemen understand that minorities have not received a fair deal in American society, but they are nonetheless offended by the militancy, and assertiveness, of them. Once again they probably reflect majority opinion. Fifty percent of the officers, compared with 40% of the Dominant public, believe minority groups in Denver are pressing too hard for their rights. Only 14% of the police and 22% of the majority public thought they were not pressing hard enough. At the same time, policemen recognize that minorities have considerable justice on their side. For example, a majority of policemen did not hold the opinion that minorities were demanding more than they had a right to. Curiously, policemen were least charitable in their judgments toward the Spanish-named. Twenty-six percent of the officers thought Negroes were demanding more than they had a right to, but 35% thought the Spanish-named were demanding more than they had a right to; only 3% thought this about Jews. Most of the officers who viewed minority demands in this light went on to say that they felt "a little angry" about it, and once again the anger was slightly greater toward the Spanish-named than toward Negroes. Interpretation of these responses is difficult. On one hand, officers may be indicating that the Spanish-named are pressing harder than the extent of their disadvantagement would warrant. On the other hand, officers may be saying that Negroes should be allowed to press harder because of personal qualities they possess in greater abundance than the Spanish-named—that they are harder-working, more intelligent, more honest, and so on. In one interpretation the police would be evaluating the extent of deprivation of each group; in the other they would be evaluating the worth of the people involved. The survey data does not allow a choice between these interpretations—all it says is that police officers believe there is more justice to the claims of Negroes than those of the Spanish-named.

While policemen are willing to concede that minority groups may have right on their side as a theoretical matter, they still resist encroachments entailed by minority demands. Their potential hostility is greater toward the encroachments of Negroes than the Spanish-named. When officers were asked whether they thought minority people were trying to push in where they were not wanted, 47% of the officers said this was true for Negroes; 17% said this was true for the Spanish-named; and 5% said this was true for Jews. The answers to this question probably indicate how the officers believe the community will react rather than the officers' own personal opinion. Negroes are the only minority group which more officers believe is resented than believe is welcomed. Three-fourths of the officers said they did not think Jews or the Spanish-named were pushing in where they were not wanted. As a commentary on the receptivity of the community to assertive actions of various minority groups, the officers' estimations are probably correct.

Testifying about their own feelings concerning minorities pushing in where they were not wanted, 19% of the officers said that in the case of Negroes this bothered them a little. Not one said it bothered him a great deal. Concerning the Spanish-named, 1% said they were bothered a great deal; 7% said they were bothered a little. In the case of Jews, only 2% said they were bothered a little; none was bothered a great deal.

Police do not have much sympathy for the leaders of

movements to improve the position of minorities. Indeed, they seem to believe that civil rights workers are unalterably antipolice. Asked to evaluate the groups policemen considered the most cooperative, civil rights workers were put at the bottom of the list, next to the unemployed. Furthermore, when civil rights workers were compared with social workers and municipal, state, and federal employees with respect to being sympathetic to policemen, civil rights workers were rated the least sympathetic.

Police officers participate less actively than the general public in organizations designed to improve the life of minority groups. Ninety-five percent of the police officers said they did not belong to such organizations, as opposed to 16% among Dominants, 17% among Negroes, and 5% among the Spanish-named. This discrepancy is probably a result of two factors. First, policemen are very wary about joining private associations, and sometimes they are even officially discouraged from doing so. Since they must regulate the society in which they live, they fear becoming compromised by involvement. Second, many of the private associations that members of the public took pride in saying they belonged to probably make very little substantive contribution to solving minority problems. The public probably overestimates the number of organizations which actually do anything of importance for minority groups.

The question that arises is whether particular policemen by virtue of background and education are better able to empathize with minority people and thus are more willing to understand minority problems. The data from our survey bears out the point that the racial schism in American society is real and deep. But perhaps certain kinds of individuals have a greater capacity for sympathetically understanding minority psychology and could, therefore, more easily bridge the experiential gap between minorities and majority. Such people, if they exist, could be invaluable in a police force. Conversely, if there are people who are peculiarly unable to empathize with minorities they should be tagged and avoided in recruitment or given special remedial attention during training.

Some scholars have suggested that lower-class individuals have greater difficulty putting themselves in other people's shoes than do higher-class individuals.[1] Policemen, coming by-and-large from upper-lower-class or lower-middle-class homes, would thus not be particularly distinguished by their ability to empathize. Nor are they particularly well equipped by education to know a great deal about minorities. For the most part they are high-school graduates with perhaps a year or two of college. One could argue, therefore, that police departments should make a greater effort to recruit higher-status individuals, with more education, thus enhancing the likelihood of finding people who are inclined to be sympathetic and open-minded about minorities. However, the ability to empathize is also affected by the similarity in background of the people involved. College graduates from upper-middle-class homes cannot readily understand the problems of a Negro family living on three thousand dollars a year. Perhaps, therefore, policemen should be from the social class of people with whom they must deal most frequently. It may be easier, for example, for a policeman with no more than a high-school education from an upper-lower-class home to understand the problems of a Negro high-school dropout, even across the barrier of race, than

[1] For a discussion of this point see McNamara, in Bordua (ed.), *op. cit.*, pp. 200-202.

for a college graduate from a professional home to do so. Even, therefore, if conclusions about the effect of class status upon the ability to empathize are correct, it is not at all clear what the police should do to their recruitment policies. They may gain as well as lose from either keeping standards as they are or raising them.

Analysis of the police and public responses shows no association between prejudice toward minority groups and sympathy for their demands, on the one hand, and background characteristics, on the other. There is no evidence that education or income affect the amount of prejudice or sympathy shown. Prejudice as well as sympathy for the demands of minorities are distributed evenly throughout the various classes of Dominant society. This study indicates, therefore, that the Police Department cannot appreciably lessen the psychological gap between policemen and minority people by means of changes in recruitment policy. Within the limits of this research instrument, the conclusion is that training after recruitment and not a change in recruitment itself must be looked to in order to affect the predispositions of policemen toward minorities.

POLICE KNOWLEDGE OF MINORITIES

Denver policemen are not well equipped through upbringing to have a great deal of personal knowledge of minority people and their problems. Their greatest handicap is the fact that they are for the most part Dominants— only about 2% of the force is Negro or Spanish-named.

Denver policemen do not come from communities where minority people are common. Two out of every five officers grew up in Denver; another 28% grew up in medium-sized western cities such as Colorado Springs, Cheyenne, Grand Junction, Abilene, and Rapid City. These places are not likely to be ethnic "melting pots." At the same time, opportunity for intense displays of race prejudice would not be common either in these cities. Only 19% of the officers said there were "many" Negroes in the place they grew up. Twenty-seven percent said there were "a few." Spanish-named people were more in evidence. Twenty-nine percent of the officers said there were "many" Spanish-named people in their home town; 25% said there were "a few." Thirty-five percent of the officers said there were no Negroes where they grew up and 30% said there were no Spanish-named persons. Thus, even if the officers had been equipped by class, education, or personal motivation to associate with Negroes or the Spanish-named, very few would have had an opportunity to do so.

One can assume, in lieu of direct evidence, that Denver policemen are not equipped by formal education to understand the problems of minority groups. While most policemen hold a high-school diploma, very few finished college. Curricula in American high schools and during the early years of college do not contain many courses on race and minority problems and certainly such courses as these are not required of students. Educational institutions are coming under increasing criticism for this lack. It has recently been pointed out that minorities are completely overlooked in American history courses. When they are mentioned it is done offhandedly, as for example in connection with the emancipation of slaves during the Civil War, the defeat of the American Indian, and the waves of immigration in the late nineteenth and early twentieth centuries. American education as a whole has failed to provide a base of information and analysis that would allow people to understand the unrest, distrust, and hostility characterizing minority-majority relations today. Policemen are products of this neglect.

Policemen do not think of themselves as being uninformed about minority problems. Quite the contrary, they consider themselves to be better informed than most people in the community. And in this assessment they are probably correct. Moreover, the basis for their understanding, contrary to that of the public generally, is personal experience. When asked to state where they got their information about some point concerning minority demands or problems, policemen invariably mentioned personal experiences. The Dominant public, by contrast, specified newspapers, radio, and TV. Policemen are conscious of being more in contact with minority problems than the rest of the community, and by virtue of the most persuasive of all teachers, namely, personal observation. Students of police relations with minority groups must realize that, while police conclusions about minorities may be colored by their professional perspectives, they have far more firsthand information than members of almost any other occupation.

We have no direct information on the amount of contact policemen have with Negroes and the Spanish-named in proportion to Dominants. The authors believe it is fair to say that contact with minority people is a daily occurrence for most officers. Contacts with minority people are of course more common in certain police districts. But since officers are rotated among districts, all policemen have a considerable number of personal experiences with Negroes and the Spanish-named to support whatever percepts they may have developed subjectively.

Police contact with minority people outside the line of

duty is also fairly common. Forty-seven percent of the officers said they had off-duty contact with Negroes; 70% had such contact with Spanish-named people. As one would expect, most of the off-duty contacts were formal ones with minority teachers, municipal employees, salesmen, and clerks. Still, 18% of the officers said they had Negro friends to whom they could say what they really thought. Only 1% of the officers said, however, that a Negro lived within a block or two of his house. Eight percent of the officers said they had Negro friends with whom they socialized by going out together or entertaining in their homes. Off-duty contacts with Spanish-named individuals were more intimate than with Negroes. Forty-four percent said they had Spanish-named friends with whom they could be completely frank; and 33% said they socialized with Spanish-named people. While this testimony by policemen cannot be accepted uncritically, it does show that many officers believe they have ample personal reasons for concluding they know something about minority people.

The vast majority of Denver policemen have worked with a Negro or Spanish-named officer. Eighty-eight percent said they had worked with a Negro; 92% with a Spanish-named officer. We do not know, however, the precise nature of the working relation of how long it lasted. It seems improbable that the 22 minority policemen on the Denver force could work very closely with 90% of the 822 white officers. That would mean they had "worked with" 740 officers. None of the officers said they were bothered at all by working with a Spanish-named policeman; 4% said they were bothered "a little" by working with a Negro. Eighty-four percent said they were not bothered at all by working with a Negro.

The amount of formal training recruits to the Denver force receive in minority problems is negligible. In 1966-67, when this study was made, recruits received 440 hours of instruction in all phases of police work in a 12-week period. According to official police figures, over 10% of that (47 hours) was devoted to community relations. Examination of the training curriculum shows, however, that very few of the offerings under community relations have anything to do with minority problems and perspectives. In fact, only slightly more than seven hours are devoted to minority problems as such. For three and one-half hours recruits met with the Director of the Denver Commission on Human Rights. One and one-half hours were devoted to a discussion of the Community Relations Office of the Police Department. One morning (3:30 hours) was given to a lecture and discussion of police sociology problems. The remainder of the 47 advertised hours of training in community relations was made up out of courses in press relations (0:50), protective services for children (2:40), juvenile psychology (3:30), handling the mentally ill (3:30), emergency obstetrics (0:50), labor relations (0:50), a tour of juvenile hall (1:40), and so forth. In short, departmental training of policemen is devoted almost exclusively to practical aspects of how to function as a police officer. Most of what passes for training in community relations is designed to teach policemen how to cope with effects and not to understand more deeply what it is that they are confronting. No attempt at all is made to instruct policemen in the psychology of minority groups or the factors that underlie minority behavior. Officers are neither trained nor particularly encouraged to re-examine police-minority relations in a stratified society and to create imaginative new approaches to the vexing problems confronting police and community alike.

The Denver situation is not unique. Very few departments make more than a token attempt to provide substantive knowledge of minority problems. Although the President's Commission on Law Enforcement and Criminal Justice recommended that courses be given in the psychology of prejudice, the background of the civil rights movement, and the history of the Negro in the United States,[2] the Commission wondered out loud whether patchwork courses tacked onto police-training programs could really do the job. Perhaps, the Commission suggested, understanding of minority perspectives can only be attained through the "kind of broad general knowledge that higher education imparts.[3] If it is true that meaningful knowledge about minority problems can be obtained best through higher education, then police departments will be obliged to reconsider their recruitment standards with respect to higher education. And they may not only need to demand college diplomas as a criterion for entrance but particular kinds of course-preparation as well. In this connection it is only fair to add that American universities might profitably ask whether they are doing an adequate job of educating students in minority history, psychology, and problems. Are they turning out the kinds of people police departments need?

The Commission summarizes its finding about knowledge of minorities by police officers as follows: "A lack of understanding of the problems and behavior of minority groups is common to most police departments and is a

[2] *The Challenge of Crime in a Free Society,* p. 102.
[3] *Ibid.,* p. 197.

serious deterrent to effective police work in the often turbu-
lent neighborhoods where [minority] groups are segregated."[4]
To this we would add one comment: *recruits* can be treated
properly as persons who have almost no knowledge of
minority problems; *experienced officers,* however, should
not be looked upon as empty vessels to be filled with the
formal facts of classroom instruction. As our study has
shown, officers are in a position to have observed and
learned a good deal about minority people. Their problem
is not an absence of information but an inability, partly as
a function of lack of time, to digest that material successfully and to draw from it lessons relevant to police-minority
problems. The experiences of officers contain considerable
amounts of unorganized information. Rather than being
lectured to, officers need to be given the opportunity to
work out their own solutions with the assistance of able,
well-informed, and sensitive teachers. If improvement in
police-minority relations is the objective, investment might
more profitably be made in officers with practical experience
rather than in the new recruit for whom police work and
the community are still largely unfamiliar. We support the
conclusion of the President's Commission that training,
especially of in-service men, should involve "problem-solving
seminars" in which the students contribute as much as the
instructor. The challenge is not to remake police officers
through education but to allow them to utilize their own
experiences and insights in order to ease the confrontation
between police and minorities.

By and large policemen think they know more about
what is troubling minority and poor people than does the
public as a whole. Only 13% of the officers said they knew

[4] *Ibid.,* p. 107.

nothing at all about what was bothering minorities and the poor. This is to be compared with 36%of Dominants, 16% of Negroes, and 26% of the Spanish-named. Eighty-five percent of the officers said they knew either a little bit or a lot about what was troubling these groups; 53% of Dominants knew a little or a lot, compared with 77% of the Negroes and 61% of the Spanish-named. While it would be unfair to say policemen are smug in their knowledge, they will not be talked down to about minorities and the poor. Officers have reason to think of themselves as well informed in this area. And compared to the rest of the community, they are.

It is also true that Denver policemen recognize that they have a great deal more to learn about minorities. They have a deep sense of inadequacy in handling minority problems. For example, 46% of the sample said their training involving racial and ethnic minorities was "not at all adequate," compared with 38% who said it was "fairly adequate" and only 4% who said it was "very adequate." The most common criticism of the initial training provided by the department was in the area of community relations. More officers cited this area of training as having been least helpful to them than any other. Officers indicated a strong desire to remedy the gaps in their preparation. Half of all officers said they were "very interested" in obtaining further training in minority relations; 29% said they were "fairly interested." Only 16% said they were not interested in such training.

By and large a policeman's sense of inadequacy in the area of minority relations is unassociated with his background. We do not find that home environment, personality, or police experience affect whether an officer is aware of a need for further training in human relations. Analysis does show, however, that the policemen on the street—patrolmen and sergeants—are more critical of police training in minority problems than are other ranks. These ranks, more than others, thought that their recruit training in minority relations was the least helpful part.

The amount of awareness among policemen of their inadequacy in the area of minority problems supports our contention that experienced police officers should not be looked upon as unregenerate souls beyond hope of saving for improved police-minority relations. They should be viewed as potential allies in this necessary work, allies who can bring enthusiasm and quantities of practical insights to a constructive effort to improve police-minority relations.

BEHAVIORAL PREDISPOSITIONS OF POLICEMEN TOWARD MINORITIES

It has been shown that policemen share the community's prejudices concerning minority groups, that they have some sympathy for the plight of minorities though it is not unalloyed with reservations about militancy, and that they have picked up considerable amounts of information from firsthand experience with minorities. Can one conclude from this that policemen systematically treat minorities in any particular way? For example, can one say that they treat them unfairly most of the time? The answer is no. Policemen might be prejudiced, unsympathetic, and not adequately informed about minorities, but they could still feel constrained to treat minority persons fairly. The linkage between personal attitudes and occupational behavior is not clear-cut. Professional ethics and organizational norms can offset, often to a surprising extent, the basic attitudes and predispositions of people. This is especially true in organizations, such as the police, where discipline is tight and unrelenting. What needs exploring are the implicit rules of conduct which policemen carry into contacts with minority people. It is necessary to know how policemen think Negroes and the Spanish-named ought to be treated, both from the point of view of personal morality and the successful accomplishment of police purposes. For behavioral predispositions of officers in specific situations will provide the necessary link between personality and behavior.

About a third of all police officers believe that Negroes and the Spanish-named *do* require stricter enforcement procedures than the rest of the population. Slightly more than half, it should be noted, disagreed with this assessment; they did not think that stricter enforcement procedures were needed. Analysis showed that belief in the need for stricter enforcement for minority groups was associated with the nature of the officer's duty, as well as his rank. Patrolmen, the most numerous of all ranks, are most apt to believe minority people require stricter enforcement.[5] Stricter enforcement for Spanish-named persons but not for Negroes was associated with the district to which the officer was assigned.[6] Policemen in districts with a high proportion of Spanish-named people were more likely to believe they require more stringent enforcement measures. In this case, familiarity appears to have bred strictness.[7]

[5] The chi-square value was significant at the 1% level.

[6] The chi-square value was significant at the 2% level.

[7] A field survey undertaken by the President's Commission on Law Enforcement and Criminal Justice found that more white officers exhibited prejudiced attitudes when assigned to Negro areas. In this case, familiarity bred prejudice (*Field Survey 3*, Vol. II, pp. 136-139).

There is an association between belief in stricter enforcement both for Negroes and Spanish-named people and officers' scoring on the anomie scale. The higher an officer's anomie, the more likely he is to believe that strict enforcement is required. Officers who scored higher on the prejudice scale were more apt to believe that Spanish-named persons ought to have stricter enforcement. Curiously, there was no significant association between prejudice and belief in Negroes requiring stricter enforcement. Authoritarianism was not correlative with a belief in the need for stricter enforcement. One cannot say that more authoritarian officers take a harder line with minority groups than others.

This study of policemen has produced a good deal of evidence indicating that officers are more apprehensive and suspicious in contacts with minority people than with Dominants. Their anxieties seem to be greater in minority contacts. Policemen believe they have been badly treated in the past in minority areas; that the crime rate is higher there; that they must be alert to physical danger to themselves and legal threats to their careers; and that the most unpleasant, complicated, discretionary, and emotional situations policemen must face will be encountered there. These perceptions and expectations undoubtedly lie behind the admission by almost two-thirds of all officers that ethnicity complicates the job of the policeman.

Close observers of the police in action have noted that force is more likely to be used when an officer faces danger and disrespect.[8] Officers most frequently use force to forestall a threat to themselves or to restore impugned authority.

---

[8] Skolnick, *op. cit.*, pp. 89-90; McNamara, in Bordua (ed.), *op. cit.*, p. 213; Westley, *op. cit.*, 125; Niederhoffer, *op. cit.*, Chap. 5; *Field Survey 3*, Vol. II, pp. 41-67.

If this is true, then recourse to force would be more common in minority areas because it is precisely in those neighborhoods that policemen anticipate danger and challenges to their authority. There is a strong presumption therefore that policemen are apt to be tougher and less forbearing with minority people.[9]

What must be understood, however, is that the reaction of the police is not so much a function of prejudice as it is of what they conceive to be the imperatives of the situation. They utilize force because they are policemen protecting themselves and vindicating their role rather than because they are individuals who dislike Negroes or the Spanish-named. In other words, to some extent the fault rests with the law-enforcement system and its requirements rather than with the individuals who staff it. For example, policemen are required to be "take charge guys."[10] They are trained to move into uncertain, unstable situations and prevent disorder, disruption, and bodily harm. A policeman is judged a failure if he allows situations to get out of hand. In minority neighborhoods he is confronted with a demanding task and circumstances that arouse his fears and threaten his self-esteem. A less discriminating and judicious use of force may indeed result. The primary lesson to be learned, however, is not that prejudiced policeman treat minority people unfairly, but rather that policemen, regardless of personality, often feel constrained to use physical force more commonly in minority areas than elsewhere. If a double

[9] We might add that it is not just with minority people that police are apt to be tougher. Young men regardless of ethnicity are often perceived to be dangerous. Policemen are wary of young men as they are of minority persons.

[10] Niederhoffer, *op. cit.*, p. 151.

standard in the use of force by policemen is to be eliminated, attention must be given not only to personalities but also to ordering the goals which are to be achieved by policemen in minority areas.

A larger question arises as to the extent to which the community as a whole, including minorities, finds the use of force and physical restraint repugnant. It is not only policemen who feel that certain groups or kinds of people deserve stricter enforcement. And it is not only policemen who find that disrespect for law and its custodians demands forceful, punitive, corrective action. The kind of guidelines the community provides for policemen, implictly and explicitly, critically affect what they will do in the heat of the moment.

What has been shown, then, is that police do carry certain predispositions into their contacts with minority people, especially in minority neighborhoods, that can produce a double standard in enforcement behavior. There is another side to the story, however. Prejudices and predispositions of a particular kind do not invariably produce systematic mistreatment and partiality. In many instances these root attitudes may work in favor of minority individuals by sparing them the full exactions of the law. Policemen are sometimes more tolerant of misbehavior by minority people, particularly if directed at their own kind, than from Dominants. Many times policemen do not take action because they feel it will do little good or that the people in the area do not really care. A brawl on the street in a minority neighborhood may result in a verbal warning; the same occurrence in a Dominant neighborhood would produce an arrest. Of course while the minority individual is spared police attention, the minority community suffers less efficient policing.

Many civil rights leaders have noted this phenomenon and have called upon the police to eliminate a double standard in enforcement conscientiousness as well as in enforcement manner.

The case has been made that the attitudes and predispositions of policemen could produce a difference in behavior toward minorities and Dominants. This is not the same as saying that policemen always do treat minority people unfairly or even that they do much of the time. In order to determine what the texture of police relations is in fact, a careful study of a cross-section of contacts as they occur would have to be undertaken. This has not been done in this book. Field surveys conducted for the President's Commission on Law Enforcement and Criminal Justice found that Negroes were not treated worse than Dominants in Boston, Chicago, and Washington, D.C. If anything, they were treated better. Negroes were, however, treated more bureaucratically, with less positive good humor and regard. "Analysis revealed no striking differences in 'unprofessional' police conduct by race or social class of the citizens. If anything, police officers appear less hostile and brusque toward Negroes and to ridicule them less often than whites.[11] In fact the Commission, after studying the many field reports, concluded that "any generalization about how 'policemen' treat 'minority-group members,' or vice versa, is almost sure to be misleading."[12]

It is apparent in Denver that police officers are aware that minority people, especially Negroes, can threaten their own careers. Presumably this would inhibit tendencies toward injudicious action. They recognize as well that

[11] *Field Survey 3*, Vol. II, p. 32.
[12] *The Challenge of Crime in a Free Society*, pp. 99-100.

police-minority relations are strained. To protect the force as well as themselves, they might hesitate to behave in such a fashion as to make minority hostility greater. The point is that prejudices and behavioral predispositions can be offset; they should not be thought of as factors which invariably determine an officer's behavior in all circumstances.

Perhaps the most important factor offsetting an officer's personal prejudices as well as his predispositions to act is the discipline of the organization. A police department activated by a broad-minded philosophy of impartiality, which demonstrates that it will demand stern adherence to its precepts, can significantly modify the professional activity of its members. Police officers function within a system of rewards and punishments—a system which is more rigid than in most occupations. The organization is itself a lever which can be used to refashion behavior, even among men who have inherited dislikes and who have punitive notions of social control. It is possible for police organizations, provided they have the will, to overcome the propensities of the men they recruit and train. Policemen can be better than the community, even though they are representative of the community. As Jerome Skolnick has said: "In sum, neither philosophical principle nor personal prejudices should be taken as the most significant factors for understanding police conduct on the job. Their actual behavior seems to be influenced more than anything else by an overwhelming concern to show themselves as competent craftsmen."[13] This is exactly what was found in Denver. Policemen want first of all to be regarded as people who do a difficult job well. The arbiters of craftsmanship are firstly leaders within the police organization and secondly the community as a whole. If

[13] Skolnick, *op. cit.,* p. 111.

notions of excellence involve impartiality, forbearance, solicitude, and humor as well as marksmanship, report writing, and number of arrests, the behavior of individual policemen will quickly reflect them.

CONCLUSION

The policeman enters into contacts with minority people holding the stereotypes and prejudices of the community as a whole. His experiences on the force have taught him to be wary of minority encounters, to be alert for violence, and to expect resentment. He is unsure of himself in contacts with them, both because he feels he does not understand them well enough and because they present him with very difficult discretionary choices. He wants to understand them better but is unsure where to turn for help. He is inclined to believe that minority people require stricter enforcement than Dominants and to discount the many charges made against the police by them. He believes the police are better than minority people say, but he is also aware that police behavior may sometimes be rude, partial, and injudicious. Policemen are knowledgeable far beyond the average about minority problems, though their knowledge is largely unorganized and unexamined. As a result, rather than drawing upon their experiences creatively they use them to reinforce accepted views. At the same time, because their knowledge is based on personal experience, it does contain more subtlety than opinions generally held in the Dominant community. Policemen understand that the lot of minority people is unenviable, but they are put off by the assertiveness of minorities, possibly because restiveness can threaten social order, which the policeman is charged with preserving. Finally, the policeman may resent minorities precisely because they demand so much of him, because they expose him to danger and self-doubt, because they threaten him and yet plead for his help, and because they continually expose the police to public scrutiny and oftentimes censure.

Improvements in police-minority relations are a matter of accommodation on both sides. The comment was made in the previous chapter that minorities are locked into an adversary relationship with the police. Furthermore, change in minority perspectives toward the police can come only as part of more fundamental changes affecting the place of minorities in the larger society. From the police side of the relationship, personal and organizational attitudes undoubtedly affect the behavior of policemen toward minorities. However, the factor most seriously inhibiting police responsiveness to the challenge of minority relations today is the failure to realize that "community relations" considerations are not extraneous to police work. Many policemen, and the public in larger measure, have not yet realized that attention to human relations can pay vast dividends in law enforcement and the defense of public safety. Many policemen are unable to see beyond the fact that demands are being made upon them by minority groups. They tend to view police reform as concessions to minorities, which implies a loss of face. Similarly from the public, voices are raised charging that any effort to palliate minority hostility causes a consequent, and equivalent, decline in standards of law enforcement. As an illustration, the decision in Denver to abolish the wearing of hard helmets as a matter of course because they were too impersonal and martial and to prohibit the carrying of nightsticks except when required was greeted with a chorus of complaints that the police were being hamstrung. The curious thing is that policemen individually understand the need for easy human relations and in their own contacts act accordingly. But as an organization they have allowed themselves to be confirmed in a relationship defined by the minorities. They have accepted the inevitability of antagonism. One result of failing to translate individual awareness and sensitivity into organizational prescriptions and public posture has been to leave the majority public uneducated and misinformed about the requirements of successful police work. What is required now of the police is the courage and imagination to realize, and preach, that increased attention to human relations is not an invidious compromise with the forces of disorder. The public especially must understand that improved relations between police and minorities will allow the police more efficiently to discharge their preeminent duty, namely, to defend and safeguard citizens from persons who are criminal, thoughtless, or irresponsible.

chapter 7

Public Order and Minority Protest

Whatever one may say about the propriety of social violence in a democracy, riots by minorities in cities of the United States have made the police a public issue. The police can no longer enjoy inconspicuousness. The riots have succeeded in dramatizing the quality of relations between police and minorities—primarily Negroes—as perceived by minorities. Minorities believe the riots show that something must be done for minorities. On the other hand, the majority community together with many minority persons are as much concerned about doing something about violence itself. These are very different points of view, leading in all probability to radically different policy prescriptions. Americans, it is fair to say, are in the process of making up their minds about the kinds of policies police departments should implement toward minority groups. What the effect of this public attention will be upon the police and upon minority relations with both the police and the majority community is an open question. One thing is sure, relations will never be the same. The real question is whether the policies adopted by the majority community will drive police and minorities closer together or further apart, with similar results for the majority-minority relations.

The purpose of this chapter is to determine likely patterns of violence in Denver. It will examine the views of various sections of the community about the likelihood of violence occurring, the issues which underlie violence, and possible participants. It will also attempt to determine which groups in Denver are the most violence-prone. Finally, nonviolent protests and demonstrations will be studied to determine their perceived utility, their effect upon minority-majority relations, their pattern of participation, and their relation to violence.

It should be said at the outset that we are in no position to make a prediction about the likelihood of rioting by Negroes or the Spanish-named. But we can assess opinions on this possibility held by different sections of the populace. Furthermore by analyzing who is likely to participate in riots and what issues seem to be related to their outbreak, we can provide information about critical issues and critical people in the generation of violence.

POSSIBILITY OF VIOLENCE

Just over half of the police officers, members of the Dominant majority, and Negroes believe that violence is unlikely in Denver. Only 41% of the police, 34% of the Dominants, and 31% of the Negroes believe there is a pretty good chance of its occurring. Spanish-named people seem to be more convinced of the likelihood of violence. Only 39% said it was unlikely, compared to 44% who said there was a good chance of its occurring. Denver police shared the assessment of Dominants and Negroes, except that a higher proportion of them rated the chances of violence occurring as being higher than had other groups. Whereas only 5% of Dominants and 7% of Negroes thought violence was very likely, 15% of the officers held this opinion.[1]

Background characteristics of individuals pertaining to class and personality do not play a role in shaping opinions about the likelihood of violence. At least they do not do so across ethnic lines. Among Dominants, for example, class in no way affects estimations. Only the personality variable of anomie has an effect. In this case people who are more anomic—that is, less optimistic about the future and their ability to influence it—are the ones who are more apt to believe violence likely. Among Negroes there is an association between assessments of violence occurring, on the one hand, and occupation and income, on the other. The higher the occupational status and the income of the respondent, the more likely he is to predict that violence is likely to occur.[2] Among Spanish-named people, only education is associated with assessments of violence. People with a great deal of education or very little of it were least convinced that violence is likely. Spanish-named persons with some

[1] The results from the intensive survey of minority groups coincided almost exactly with results from the general public survey. In both surveys Spanish-named people were more convinced than Negroes that violence was likely.

[2] The chi-square value was significant at the 5% level.

high school or with a high-school diploma tend in greater proportions to believe violence is likely. There is some evidence for the conclusion, therefore, that among minority people higher class status contributes to an assessment that social violence is likely. This association may simply mean that such people are apt to be in closer touch with social life in their communities. It may also mean that they either fear such an outbreak more than others or would welcome such an outbreak more than others, perhaps because they feel more intensely the gap between achievement and status. Later we will present evidence designed to demonstrate whether class does affect the violence-proneness of minority people, and that will help to resolve this point.

Policemen as well as members of the public link the outbreak of violence with Negroes. Respondents were asked to specify where a riot would break out, and all of them specified Negro sections of the city.[3] However, whereas Dominants and the Spanish-named cited depressed Negro ghettos, policemen and Negroes themselves said that a riot was more likely in the more well-to-do Negro residential areas, such as Park Hill and around Dahlia Shopping Center. Negroes and police officers seem to recognize that social violence is not produced by a simple identity between ethnicity and depressed economic circumstances. Dominants and the Spanish-named do not appear to realize this. Or, Negroes and police may be in closer touch with community sentiment, knowing that within the past two summers there has been considerably more overt unrest at the Dahlia area than in Five Points. Whatever the explanation, policemen and Negroes are in general agreement about where violence is likely to occur. Moreover, their opinions differ signifi-

[3] Such as Park Hill, Five Points, and Dahlia Shopping Center.

cantly from those of other groups in the community not directly involved.

There is a very significant difference in opinion among various sectors of the populace concerning the causes of urban riots. Negroes list the primary cause as inequality and discrimination; Spanish-named people agree. Negroes list police brutality in second place among causes; Spanish-named people list unemployment second and police brutality third. Dominants, on the other hand, list outside agitators, Communists, and troublemakers as the primary cause—one out of every three Dominants believes this. In short, where minorities perceive their own grievances as the immediate cause, Dominants look for human agency in the form of irresponsible or subversive individuals. If these differing viewpoints are not reconciled, violence is going to produce an increased polarization in view between majority and minority. Dominants will seek to meet violence with punitive sanctions directed against individuals; minorities will continually wonder why violence is not met with structural solutions to fundamental problems.

The police are not as unaware as Dominants that police behavior is an important factor in causing violence. Over one out of three officers said that an arrest or an incident involving the police was likely to spark riots.[4] Only 10% of the officers specified outside influences as the immediate cause of riots. At the same time, officers did not forget outside agitators, 13% saying that they were a specific catalyst of violence. Officers were inclined to view this factor as being

[4] There is ample evidence for this. The McCone Report on the Watts riots, for example, found that of seven riots in eastern cities in 1964 and 1965 all had started over a police incident. Subsequent riots have followed the same scenario (Governor's Commission on the Los Angeles Riots, *Violence in the City—An End or a Beginning?* p. 28).

more important than material and social advancement. In fact, fully a third of all officers said they did not think Denver minorities suffered from disabilities which were perceived to be so serious as to produce rioting.

Policemen see the immediate causes of riots more like minorities do than the Dominant community does. They are agonizingly aware of the sensitivity of their own position. However, like the Dominant majority, policemen tend to downplay impersonal factors having to do with discrimination and material progress and to dwell on human agency. Negroes and the Spanish-named, by contrast, want the world to know that violence grows out of minority status. Agitators, for them, are like froth on the wave.

PATTERNS OF PARTICIPATION

At the time of writing, late winter 1968, Denver had not yet been the scene of a riot. Once or twice during past summers young Negroes had congregated, a few rocks and bottles were thrown, and a Molotov cocktail was hurled at a storefront. But a full-scale riot never broke out; milling never gave way to violence. As a result, this study was unable to analyze the backgrounds and formative experiences of participants in violence. The researchers were forced to rely on a projective question in order to determine how willing different people might be to participate in violent riots.

Members of the public were asked how they felt about riots and violence that resulted from civil rights demonstrations and marches. The vast majority of people, regardless of ethnicity, said they were upset by them. Only a very small

proportion said that riots and violence pleased them. Dominants and the Spanish-named were in almost complete agreement, with Negroes being slightly more favorably disposed
toward violence. Only 1% of the Dominants and the Spanish-
named were pleased by violence, as opposed to 3% of the
Negroes. Ninety-three percent of Dominants, 88% of the
Spanish-named, and 86% of the Negroes said they were
upset by rioting. The residue in each sample had no clear
opinion. The intensive study of minority people produced
slightly different results. It has already been shown that
responses given during intensive interviews tended to be
more negative, more forthright in criticism, than responses
from the general public survey. In the intensive survey 6%
of Negroes said they were pleased by violence, compared
with 3% of them in the general public survey. Only 77%
of the Negroes in the intensive survey said they were upset
by violence. Results for Spanish-named people coincided
exactly between the two surveys.

We may say, therefore, that Negroes are slightly more
favorably disposed toward violence than Dominants or the
Spanish-named, but that the vast majority of every ethnic
group is upset by it.

Minority people in the intensive survey were also asked
directly whether they, or members of their immediate
family, would get involved in a riot if one broke out in
Denver. The results are disquieting, for they indicate that
for many minority people the temptation to get involved in
a riot is considerable. Twenty-eight percent of the Negroes
and 17% of the Spanish-named said they—or someone in
their family—would get involved if a riot broke out. Fifty-
seven percent of the Negroes and 73% of the Spanish-named
said they would not get involved. One sees again that vio-

lence is more appealing to Negroes than to the Spanish-
named.

It would be reasonable to expect that different kinds
of people within ethnic groups would feel differently about
violence. One might think that more highly educated people
or people with higher incomes might be less likely to participate in violence. This does not appear to be the case.
There are no significant associations between background
variables and being pleased by the prospect of violence.
Income, education, sex, age, years in Denver, and so forth,
do not affect the dispositions of people toward violence.
One cannot say, for example, that the greater the poverty
of a Negro the more violence-prone he will be. Nor can
statements like this be made for Dominants or the Spanish-
named. In our study, and based on a single projective question about approval of violence, the only variable that plays
a determining role in disposing people to violence is ethnicity. It overrides any other parameter of social status.

The incident which has most commonly provided the
spark igniting riots in urban America has been a contact
between police and minority people. This study has already
shown that "police brutality" is listed by minority people as
one of the primary causes of urban riots. It seems reasonable
to expect, therefore, that people who look favorably upon
violence have had unpleasant experiences with the police or
hold markedly critical attitudes toward them. The data do in
fact show that negative reactions to the police are associated
with the approval of violence, although analysis does not
show that unpleasant experiences at the hands of the police
are correlative with approval of violence. The failure to find
a clear association between personal experiences and approval of violence is due partly to the projective nature of

the question and partly to its phraseology. Respondents were asked how they reacted to civil rights marches and demonstrations that turned into riots. Specifically, were they upset or pleased? In order to get precisely at their reactions to urban violence, they should have been asked about violence in minority ghettos without reference to civil rights protests. Therefore, answers to the question may not reveal adequately whether people approve or disapprove of the urban violence of America's recent long hot summers. And, furthermore, the absence of clear association between approval-disapproval on this item and unpleasant experiences with the police may not indicate that such experiences do not play a critical role. A person could be upset by violence growing out of civil rights tactics and still have had unpleasant experiences himself that might lead him to want to participate in a riot if one broke out. As will be shown in a moment, there is a very clear association between participating in nonviolent agitational activities and unpleasant experiences, which creates the presumption that the same would be true with respect to violent activities. This presumption is strengthened by one bit of direct evidence. Among all ethnic groups, people who have had a friendly talk with a policeman are much less likely to approve of violence than those who have not. Putting the matter the other way around: people who approve of violence are much less likely to have had friendly personal relations with a policeman.[5]

Even though the question about the approval of vio-

[5] Chi-square values were significant at the 5% level for all ethnic groups. Of Negroes who had a friendly talk with policemen, 97.9% were upset by violence and 2.1% could not make up their minds. Among Negroes who had not had a friendly talk, however, only 85.5% were upset by violence; 14.2% could not make up their minds. In neither group did anyone say they approved of violence.

lence left something to be desired, it could be used to show an association between reactions to demonstrations that go violent and evaluations of the police. To illustrate, Negroes who do not condemn violence tended to believe that the reputation of the police was very low in the neighborhood, that their neighborhood receievd worse police service than elsewhere, and that they themselves had reason to be dissatisfied with the way police had responded to a call. Spanish-named people who did not disapprove of violence tended very strongly to believe that the police treated minorities unfairly. Ninety-seven percent of the Spanish-named people who thought the police were always or usually fair to minorities also condemned civil rights demonstrations that became violent. Only 72% of those who thought police treatment was often unfriendly actually condemned violence stemming from civil rights agitations.

The direction of cause and effect, if any, between the condemnation of violence and evaluations of the police cannot be determined from the data. All that can be said is that people's attitudes toward violence seem to be related to a posture toward the police. The data supports the finding in the Watts riot that people who participate in violence tended to believe that the police mistreat minorities.[6] The police do play a different role in the perceptual and evaluative world of the person who participates in violence than in the world of those who do not.

NON-VIOLENT AGITATION

Although "violence in the streets" has become a preoccupation of politicians and the majority public, it is a

[6] *Task Force Report: The Police*, p. 148.

relatively new form of minority militancy. The standard techniques of persuasion until roughly 1964 were studiously nonviolent, taking the form of boycotts, public meetings, marches, and an open but selective breaking of discriminatory laws. The Montgomery bus boycott, 1956, the massive march on Washington, 1963, and the sit-ins of the early 1960's typified protest activities in the earlier phase. In the national concern with urban violence, one is apt to forget that enormous restraint had been shown by minorities for a very long time. This does not, of course, justify violence. It may, however, help to explain it. Whether violence will give way to nonviolent tactics remains to be seen. But it is important to avoid thinking of all militancy as if it were violent, and thereby neglect to study the support for nonviolent protests among various segments of the population.

The rate of participation in civil rights demonstrations and marches is much higher than the incidence of violence-proneness, regardless of ethnic group. The highest participation rate is shown by Negroes—19%; among Spanish-named the proportion was half as great—9%; and among Dominants one-sixth as great—3%. Just as the vast majority of the population do not respond favorably to the prospect of violence, so the vast majority do not participate actively in public demonstrations of any kind. A larger number of people have considered participating and presumably are not totally averse to doing so at some time. Six percent of Dominants, 29% of Negroes, and 22% of the Spanish-named said they had considered taking part in a civil rights demonstration.

Among Dominants and Negroes younger people are more apt to have participated than others. This is not true of the Spanish-named. Indeed, among them analysis shows no association between participation and social position, education, sex, and so forth. Nor, for that matter, among Negroes, is any background variable except age associated with participation. The willingness to participate in civil rights demonstrations is evenly distributed among Negroes and the Spanish-named; it is not affected by material achievement, professional status, or even the sex of respondents. This is not true for Dominants. Age, occupation, and education are associated with different rates of participation. Participation is greatest among Dominants who are young, well educated, and in business and clerical occupations. The older a person is, the less education he has, and the more menial his occupation, the less likely he is to have participated in a public demonstration. This is also true for Dominants who have ever thought of participating, except that women are more likely to have considered participating than men.

The data shows, then, that Negroes and the Spanish-named regardless of background are more likely to have participated in civil rights demonstrations than Dominants and that the willingness of Dominants to do so is affected by their age, education, and occupation.

At the same time, there is a dramatic difference in opinion between Dominants and Negroes about whether they approve nonviolent demonstrations. Most Dominants do *not* approve demonstrations and marches, even though they are nonviolent. Sixty-two percent disapproved; 29% approved. Most Negroes do approve of nonviolent demonstrations and marches. Seventy-two percent approved; 22% disapproved. In other words, Negroes and Dominants are diametrically opposed in their views about peaceful demonstrations. Curiously, the Spanish-named line up beside the Dominants in this matter. More of them disapprove peaceful demonstrations than approve them—45% to 38%. For some reason, Dominants and the Spanish-named disapprove of any attempt by Negroes to command public attention and influence policy through the exercise of nonviolent group activities undertaken in public. The irony of the situation is that where Dominants certainly are strongly opposed to violence perpetrated by Negroes in support of their rights, the majority of Dominants are also opposed to Negroes campaigning against their status by nonviolent means. This does not mean that most Dominants would support the brutal or illegal repression of nonviolent minority demonstrations; they probably would not. But it does mean that they are not sympathetic to visible, public campaigns to redress minority grievances and status.

Policemen exhibit greater sympathy toward nonviolent marches and demonstrations than does the Dominant majority. More police favor nonviolent demonstrations than condemn them. Forty-six percent approved, 38% disapproved, and 15% could not make up their minds.

The Dominant majority and the Spanish-named also agreed that nonviolent demonstrations and marches did more harm than good. The proportions were very similar to the answers from the approve-disapprove question. In this case policemen agree with the Dominant public: 65% thought they did more harm than good; 21% thought they did more good than harm. Negroes thought nonviolent demonstrations did have utility; 69% thought they did good; 16% thought they did harm.

Among Negroes and the Spanish-named, approval of nonviolent demonstrations and considerations of their utility are not affected by social background. Income, education, sex, and occupation do not affect the views of minority people toward nonviolent demonstrations. Among Dominants, only occupation is associated with approval of nonviolent demonstrations and the belief that they are useful. People in service occupations and professions are most inclined to believe that nonviolent demonstrations do more good than harm. Laborers, business people, and the unemployed are most critical of the utility of demonstrations. By-and-large, however, regardless of ethnic group, attitudes toward nonviolent demonstrations are unaffected by the background of individuals.

What a person thinks of nonviolent demonstrations and whether he has participated in them is very definitely linked to his views of and experiences with the police. In other words, within ethnic groups, relations with the police—both psychological and actual—are much more important in determining an individual's posture toward demonstrations than is achievement and social status. For example, for Dominants, Negroes, and the Spanish-named, approval of nonviolent demonstrations is associated[7] with the belief that policemen treat minorities unfairly. Among Dominants and the Spanish-named, belief in the usefulness of nonviolent demonstrations is linked to the view that charges of police brutality are mostly true.[8] The evidence from an analysis of the data on participation in demonstrations is even more convincing. Among all ethnic groups, people who have participated in a demonstration are much more likely to have had someone in their immediate family mistreated by the police than people who have not joined a demonstration. For example, 35% of the Negroes who had demonstrated belonged to families in which someone had been

[7] The Chi-square value was significant at the 5% level.
[8] The Chi-square value was significant at the 5% level.

abused by the police. Among nonparticipating Negroes, only 17% belong to families where someone had been abused by the police. Again, 5% of Negroes who participated thought the reputation of the police was high, while 12% thought it was low. Among nonparticipating Negroes, 32% thought it was high and 8% thought it was low. For Dominants and the Spanish-named, there is an association[9] between having had personal experience with police mistreatment of minorities and participating in civil rights demonstrations. Likewise, belief that charges of police brutality are mostly true is linked to participation, at least for Dominants and the Spanish-named.[10]

Furthermore, people of every ethnic group who have participated tend also to be the kind of people who have made a complaint against the police. This would indicate either that participators are simply activists, whatever the mode, or that they have in fact had more things to complain about.

The evidence is overwhelming that participants in civil rights demonstrations tend to share unfavorable views of the police, as well as to have had more unpleasant personal experiences with the police than nonparticipators. While it would be a mistake to conclude that improvement in police relations with the public would discourage civil rights agitation, there is no doubt that police relations with the public are very much on the minds of civil rights demonstrators. The police are an important target of agitation and are perceived as a primary grievance among people concerned with civil rights matters.

This is also true for people who have considered taking

[9] The Chi-square value was significant at the 5% level.
[10] The Chi-square value was significant at the 5% level.

an active role in demonstrations but have not yet taken the plunge. Would-be participatnts from the Negro and Spanish-named communities tend to have had unpleasant personal experiences at the hands of the police, to have given thought to complaining about their behavior (although not actually having done so), and to believe that brutality is a fundamental cause of riots.[11]

PREVENTION OF VIOLENCE

There is no doubt that with respect to protest and potential violence, Negroes are the critical minority group in Denver. Spanish-named people tend, like Dominants, to deprecate the value and propriety of any kind of public protest. It must also be stressed that outright violence is not approved by large numbers of Negroes. Although Negroes approve it in higher proportions than other groups, they by and large are appalled by it. Policemen, as well as the majority community, should not forget this fact, for it has important implications for the way in which violence should be handled. The majority community could make no greater mistake than to lump all Negroes together concerning their willingness to engage in and support violence.

Violence in American cities is not only a symptom of the alienation of Negroes from society; it is also a cause of increased alienation by virtue of producing a more extreme polarization of views between Dominants and minorities. Negroes, supported by the Spanish-named, believe that the fundamental cause of unrest is discrimination, which produces inadequate employment opportunities, substandard housing, poor education, and inferior medical care. Their

[11] The Chi-square value was significant at the 5% level.

prescription for preventing further violence therefore encompasses ambitious and costly programs designed to overcome structural rigidities in the provision of equal opportunities to minority people. Dominants, on the other hand, when they give attention to preventing violence do not think of structural solutions but in terms of constraining the human agents of violence. Dominants and minorities are not on the same wavelength when it comes to recommending solutions to the common problem which violence is. The tragedy is that failure to agree on solutions to violence will fan the flames of violence. For the failure to agree on solutions will dramatize, as much as the violence, the chasm separating black from white, minority from majority.

In striving to eliminate or contain violence, the dominant community must be particularly careful to avoid the pitfall of equating every demonstration with violence. The majority community must be discriminating enough to realize that while demonstrations may indeed be a breeding ground for violence, they are also an alternative to violence. Indeed, if in choking off violence the majority community also represses demonstrations, they may very well reap the whirlwind. This danger is not academic. Our study has shown that Dominants condemn violence and at the same time do not favor nonviolent demonstrations and marches. Dominants, it would appear, are made acutely uncomfortable by minority protests carried on in public places. Leadership in the dominant community must exert itself to teach *majority people* that violence and protests are not the same thing; they must do this in order to keep open for minorities an alternative mode of public persuasion. Dominant leaders must be prepared to draw this distinction, which in particular cases may not be easy to do, and to teach it to their constituents even when the floodgates of violence appear to have broken, because at that moment the urge to retaliate upon all forms of minority protest will be intense.

Policemen are not particularly profound or insightful in their recommendations about how to prevent violence. Their views tend to reflect the preoccupations of their profession. For example, when asked what steps might be taken to make certain riots do not take place in Denver, the most common recommendation was something to the effect that better understanding—communication—good relations should be created between majority and minority. An equal proportion recommended more stringent enforcement, generally a "get tough" policy with people who were potentially violent. Almost a fifth of all policemen believed that nothing really could be done, that riots worked to their own logic and one could never be sure they would not break out. Only fifth in the list of recommendations were those dealing with programs designed to meet basic conditions of life, such as more jobs, better education, and organized activities for young people. It is worth noting that even fewer officers actually thought that riots could be certainly prevented by controlling agitators and outside influences. Where 9% of the officers suggested social programs as the best defense against violence, only 5% cited particular attention to agitators. It is possible, of course, that some of the 17% that recommended stricter law enforcement had agitators and outside influences in mind.

When officers were asked specifically what the police could do, one out of every three thought in terms of traditional police responses, such as increased patrols, more effective surveillance, and stricter and more automatic enforcement. Twenty-three percent did mention improved community relations programs and the need for better training of policemen in the problems of minority communities. One sees a suggestion once again in the data that policemen are used to thinking in particular ways but that they may be a good deal more receptive to creative innovations in police practices if they can be convinced that these innovations will be effective. There is more than a hint in our data that policemen would welcome new solutions, for they know too well the inadequacies of the old, but they have not yet been offered programs which are practical enough to command their enthusiasm.

Policemen are a critical variable in the generation of violence. They are at once the symbolic cause of violent unrest and the agency charged with restoring order. We have seen that people who approve violence and who have assumed an active role in civil rights demonstrations are apt to be less well disposed toward the police than others; moreover, that they are likely already to have had experiences at the hands of the police that they consider unjust, improper, or unfair. Policemen enter incipient riot situations with several strikes against them. It is impossible for them to rectify at a stroke the accumulated grievances of the demonstrators and potential rioters. They are speaking to people who have negative views more set than most— people who, as it were, are partially deaf. Indeed, one of the salient reasons for these people being on the street may be a deep-seated belief that police are their sworn enemies from whom they cannot expect fairness or sympathy. This being the case, the freedom for maneuver possessed by the police is likely to be very small. Their physical presence itself becomes a spark that inflames hostility. For their part, policemen are aware of the enmity they attract; they are apprehensive, alert, and unsure of themselves. They are fearful for their own safety, as well as conscious of having to protect the larger community from the depredations of the few.

Policemen are not disposed automatically to use force in order to restrain a milling crowd and quell the threat of riot. Although officers sometimes talk tough about meeting force with force and not taking a namby-pamby attitude toward would-be lawbreakers, the fact is that police shrink from the use of physical force. It spells danger to them personally and they have been taught that the successful officer is the one who achieves order with the least amount of disruption. Two-thirds of Denver officers have had the department's course in riot control training. When asked what they had learned from it, most officers mentioned psychological tactics, such as opening conversations with leaders, displaying patience, trying to understand the group's grievances, remaining calm, and showing solidarity without resort to force. Many officers are not bad amateur psychologists; they know that one does not goad a crowd.[12] But it is also true that policemen are prepared to use force to counter force when peaceful means fail. They may even feel a certain amount of righteousness in doing so, since in most cases they have tried, conscientiously, to contain violence without resort to force. It requires considerable self-control for officers to stand calmly in front of a milling throng—people openly defiant, hostile, and threatening—and engage them in protracted conversation. When such nonforceful tactics fail, policemen undoubtedly shift the blame to the

[12] See the interesting comments of Westley, *op. cit.*, 123, on the nonviolent tactics used by officers in facing hostile crowds.

crowd—not always without reason—and may release pent-up emotions through guns and clubs.

Considering the predispositions of would-be rioters toward the police it is hard for the police effectively to meet the challenge of a confrontation. If they do take the first steps toward conciliation, tremendous effort and enormous presence of mind are required. If, on the other hand, force is used and a clash not prevented, the worst opinions of the rioters and demonstrators are confirmed. The cycle of suspicion, hostility, and protest is renewed. Force certainly will not break this cycle. The tragedy is that the police often have no choice. If nonviolence fails to contain mob action, force is what the police are trained for and expected by the community to use. Like minorities, locked into a discriminatory situation despite themselves, policemen through their ubiquitous contacts with minorities serve as the symbol for majority oppression and must simultaneously contain the emotional reactions to that status. Policemen too are locked into a situation not of their making.

The data from this study demonstrate the enormous gap between majority and minority people with respect to the seriousness of minority problems and the means appropriate to their solution. Furthermore, the data show that from urban violence different groups learn very different lessons. Although our study does not allow us to say that violence will break out in Denver, it does create the strong presumption that trouble is likely. In our city, and in the country as a whole, members of the majority community are engaging in the folly of wishful thinking, founded on an appalling ignorance about minority conditions and attitudes, if they believe that violence cannot happen here or long endure.

chapter 8

Toward Improving Police- Community Relations

Relations between the police and the community, between the police and minority groups particularly, are complex and multi-faceted. Most generalizations about the relationship are inadequate because they fail to consider important dimensions of the relation or they ignore differences in point of view among participants on both sides or even of the same people in different circumstances. An axiom for all people concerned about police-community relations should be that summary judgments about the relationship put forth by spokesmen for both sides are bound to be half-truths, obscuring as much as they reveal.

Negroes and the Spanish-named in Denver are wary of the police. This is true regardless of the class of the minority-group individual. Relations with the police are uncommonly sensitive. Encounters with them are not routine happenings, as they are for most Dominants, which can be shrugged off and forgotten. Minority people are alert for signs of prejudice and partiality. They are not inclined to be charitable in their judgments about the police; they are willing to believe the worst, especially concerning charges of brutality. Because minority people are wary, they probably overdramatize what happens in contacts. Hidden meaning and motivation is sought in the most ordinary actions. The amount of direct contact between policemen and minority group individuals is not disproportionate to their numbers. They seem to request help from the police as frequently, proportionately, as majority people. At the same time, they probably call upon the police less often than circumstances warrant, that is, less often than Dominants similarly placed would do. Curiously, for example, Dominants admit to discussing problems more often with the police than do minority people. The implication is that minority people tend to avoid the police more than do Dominants, a fact which is supported by folk-wisdom within the minority communities about the advisability of not becoming involved with the police.

Minority people also desire more efficient police service. They deprecate a double standard in police operations with respect to both impartiality and conscientiousness of the police. Minority people do not want a "free ride" for minority lawbreakers. Quite the contrary, for it is minority people who suffer most from the criminal activity of minority persons. Like Dominants, minority individuals require many nonenforcement services of the police. They are particularly apt to call policemen for help with medical emergencies. Police are for them an important avenue of access to municipal services.

The police are more important for minority persons than the amount of firsthand contact would seem to justify. Police appear to have symbolic value for minorities—they stand for power and authority and are visible signs of majority domination. This perspective weighs upon all encounters between police and minorities and must be recognized and understood by anyone who would attempt to improve the quality of relations between police and minorities.

Policemen, on the other side of the relationship, are wary of minority people and unnaturally attentive to nuances in the relationship. They are suspicious of minority people, believing that they are more likely to be involved in criminal activity than Dominants. They consider violence against persons more common among minority people and are therefore more concerned for their own safety when intervening. Policemen believe that hostility is greater toward them in minority neighborhoods, and they expect a greater incidence of resistance in making arrests. Police are well aware that their relations with minority groups are volatile. For this reason they are unsure of themselves in encounters with minorities, almost desperately afraid that an ugly scene will arise. They know that if this happens they will be subjected to searching scrutiny by their superiors as well as the public and that they will be targets of intemperate criticism and even abuse. Police are apprehensive as well about minority people retaliating by threatening their livelihood through the filing of civil suits. Policemen find the calls for assistance from minority people less straightforward than those from Dominants. This is partially a result of the cultural gap between Dominant policemen and minority people. But it is also the result of the nature of the calls themselves. Calls from minority people present the officer with particularly troublesome discretionary situations, involving difficult decisions about the propriety of making an arrest and of the proper form in which assistance should be given.

All in all, officers tend to feel that the demands made upon them by minority people are particularly burdensome and the consequences of a misstep potentially very harmful. There is little doubt that policemen are put on their mettle by encounters with minority persons.

The expectations policemen have about minority people are not primarily a result of prejudiced attitudes. There may be some of this, to be sure. Policemen do share the fundamental attitudes toward minority groups of the majority community. But more important than inherited predispositions are the professional experiences and demands of police life. Policemen are required to preserve order and enforce the law. They take this charge seriously, and see situations and people through this screen of duty. Policemen, furthermore, are not uninformed about the life of minority people. Indeed, they have considerably more firsthand contact with Negroes and the Spanish-named than most people in the community. Their impressions of what is right and proper to do in contacts with minority people are based, then, on personal observations, not upon secondhand opinion. They are impatient with the uninformed comments of outside observers who have no experience of life on the streets or in the ghetto. Policemen know, better than most, that they are distrusted by minority people. They also know that minority persons expect a great deal of the police, perhaps more than Dominants. Knowing firsthand the full range of relations between police and minorities, policemen believe their stock with minority persons is not as unrelievedly low as many detractors suggest. Policemen also feel cynical, and sometimes angry, because they have been placed, despite themselves, in such an invidious position. They are asked to do a job that few people understand, involving, in the case of minority persons, people who are bitter and frustrated. The police-man's ability to reach the roots of problems is exceedingly limited; yet Dominant society expects him to contain unrest and disorder and criticizes him freely if he does it ill-consideredly, in haste, or anger. The police officer, in his relations with minority people, feels terribly put upon. He, like minority group people, feels caught in an embittering situation not of his own making—a situation few people in majority society will make the effort or have the patience to try to understand.

What can be done to ease the relations between these two groups—police, on the one hand, minorities, on the other? Are there solutions to be found which are at the same time consistent with the requirements of order in modern society and the demands for justice and self-esteem in minority groups? It is not our purpose to put forward a complete, detailed blueprint for improved police-community relations. It would be presumptuous to do so. At the same time, however, the Denver study has uncovered aspects of the police-community relationship which it would be well to underscore, for these considerations should, we believe, constrain policy-making. Indeed, if these points are forgotten, it is our opinion that the success of schemes to improve police-community relations is likely to be limited.

1. Solutions to tension between police and minorities should not be overpersonalized. There is a tendency for people to focus blame exclusively upon the actors involved. The police, some people say, are prejudiced and brutal. Other people argue that minorities are oversensitive, exaggerating "brutality" in order to embarrass majority society and enhance their own position. Views of this kind mistake the nature of the problem. There are indeed biased policemen, as there are self-seeking people among minority groups. But most policemen and most minority persons are reflecting attitudes congruent with the different worlds they inhabit. One can no more achieve a solution to police-minority antagonism by weeding out prejudiced policemen than one can eliminate urban riots by seeking out "outside agitators."

2. Policemen sincerely want to ease the tension between themselves and minority groups. Policemen are aware of the ambiguous position they occupy; they are not insensitive to what minority people think of them. Solutions to police-minority problems must be built upon the policeman's own desire for eased relationships. He must be approached as a partner in the enterprise, and not as a rogue who must be reformed despite himself. The policeman's own desire for a calmer, more secure, less uncertain relationship with minority people is an important quality to be harnessed to the task of reform.

3. If reform is to work, policemen must not be talked down to. They are exceedingly knowledgeable not only about the requirements for successful police work but about minority problems and minority perspectives on the law. Very often their insights are unorganized and unexploited, even by their own establishment. It is not only tactically unwise to treat policemen as if they were "know-nothings"; it

would waste a precious resource of information and insight.

4. Policemen, for their part, must learn the hollowness of the dictum that their exclusive duty is to enforce the law and not to become involved with social reform. Society does, of course, hold them responsible for the enforcement of law. What this view overlooks, however, is that in pursuing the primary objective a great deal more than enforcement activity is required. Policemen often put themselves in the position of seeming to be indifferent to human relations. This is a pose, and most good policemen know that it is. Few of them practice indifference of this kind on the street; to do so would be to invite trouble. Enforcement of law does indeed involve concern with and sensitivity toward social problems; moreover, policemen actually spend the larger portion of their working time in activities other than law enforcement. They play "cops and robbers" very occasionally compared with the mass of nonenforcement work they perform.

The maintenance of the hard-line enforcement posture by policemen, pretending unconcern with social problems, has resulted in a serious misunderstanding of the nature of police work by the public. It is true, as policemen frequently claim, that the public does not understand the life of a policeman and what his duties involve. But the fault is in large part the policeman's own. Policemen speak of themselves very often in terms of unrealistic stereotypes. For some reason they fear to take the public into their confidence. But if police-minority relations are going to be improved, it will only be if policemen admit among themselves and then to the public that sensitivity to social problems is a prime ingredient of successful police operations.

5. Policemen must begin openly and creatively to study

and discuss the discretionary aspects of their work. The President's Commission on Law Enforcement and Criminal Justice coined the happy phrase "unarticulated improvisation" to describe police activity. Policemen *are* decision-makers. It is in society's interest and theirs, not that discretion be eliminated, but that it be employed intelligently, sensitively, and farsightedly.

6. Ethnicity is a critical variable in determining the attitudes of people toward the police and the nature of their contacts with policemen. Indeed, compared to characteristics of social class and material success, ethnicity is the primary differentiating variable. The majority community must understand that minority group people are genuinely and seriously concerned with police activities. Majority people could make no greater mistake than to discount the importance of the police in the world of minority groups. Dominants must realize that their own experiences, as well as their own inherited perceptions of the police, are no basis for understanding how policemen appear to minority people; therefore, when issues about the police are raised by minority people—for example, involving charges of police brutality or a civilian review board—majority people must not dismiss them out of hand. An unsympathetic response will only make the gap in trust and respect greater between majority and minority.

It is true that criticisms of the police may sometimes be exaggerated or used for personal aggrandizement by minority spokesmen. Nonetheless, very few Dominants are in a position to know for sure whether what minority people assert about the police is true or false. Majority people must recognize their own inability to judge. They may properly hesitate to accept uncritically all that minority people say about the police, but they should not hesitate to display lively concern, sympathy, and a willingness to learn.

7. Policemen as well as members of the majority community must beware of accepting the quality of the relationship between themselves and minority groups as it is apt to be defined by minority people. That is, they must not fall too quickly into the habit of treating all relations with minorities as being of an adversary character. Most importantly of all, they must not turn a deaf ear upon minority grievances just because they are couched in the language of demands. And they must not assume that a gain for minorities is a loss either for the police or the majority community. It is conceivable, indeed most likely, that rectification of police-minority relations can be a gain for all concerned. The point is, though, that the opportunity to display initiative rests with the police and with majority society. It does not belong to minorities. If, therefore, police and majority individuals accept the notion of natural antagonism of interests, they will forfeit the chance to respond creatively to minority demands. They must have the vision, the magnanimity, to respond even though they are being pushed. If they are unable to do so, the loss will be everyone's.

8. Police work is necessary to society and has merit uniquely its own. Civilization and order are related, although one must be careful not to define the one exclusively in terms of the other. There is a tendency for some minority people, as well as their Dominant allies, to denigrate the entire function of the police in an understandable desire to bring about reform within the force. Neither society as a whole nor particular groups within it would profit from the destruction of an effective police organization. Argumentation should properly focus on the nature of police activity,

not on its presence or absence. It is a shortsighted strategy to try to produce reform out of virulent criticism of the police function as such. It would be wiser tactically, also, for reformers to identify with the need for policing in modern society, rather than creating a division between the supporters of reform and the supporters of the police.

9. The police cannot be expected to eliminate urban violence. They may not even be able to contain it successfully. The majority community must not become so preoccupied with meeting violence with a police response that it overlooks the deep, pervasive causes of violence. This would be to cope with symptoms only and not with causes. Moreover, the public must realize that there are limits to the ability of the police to intervene successfully to divert an incipient riot. The police are themselves catalysts of violence, and their entry into a threatening situation may make matters worse, as well as sow the seeds for future hostility between police and minority people.

10. Members of the majority community must be careful not to repress all opportunities for the display of minority militancy. They must learn to distinguish acceptable disorder from unacceptable violence. They must also learn that controlled militancy has healing power for minority participants, especially if it achieves a measure of success. Minority people do not want to be dependent upon Dominant society even for their social advancement. They want to feel that they are obtaining something through their own efforts. Dominant society must allow minority people to present demands, raucously and publicly, for two reasons: first, in order to find out what is going on within minority groups and, second, in order to provide an opportunity for minority people to share in shaping their own destiny. The end of

dependency by minorities upon Dominants undoubtedly
entails *forcing* Dominant society to do some things and not
simply waiting until Dominant society deigns to give. "Black
Power," for example, is one instance of this desire for an end
to dependency. In fact, the disenchantment that has sprung
up between many Dominant liberals and more militant
Negroes can be traced to the failure of these sympathetic
Dominants to understand that minorities want to do things
for themselves.

The fundamental theme implicit in all these observations is that solutions to police-minority antagonism must be
founded on an appreciation of the structural nature of the
problem. Policemen can be fair-minded, minority people can
be law-abiding and peaceful, and yet both can still be suspicious and critical of one another. Tension between police
and minorities is not a function simply of malevolent personalities. It is a function of different social roles and positions. Solutions must, therefore, be founded on an understanding of the structure of the worlds of the police officer
and the minority individual. The trick will be to reorder
their relationship so that the virtue of being true to one's
own kind and one's social role will produce harmony rather
than hostility.

The basic determinants of the police-minority relationship are twofold: first, the deprivation and inequality of
minority groups and, second, the imperatives of the police
function. Most people would probably agree that a lessening
of tension bought at the expense of order would be too dear
as well as ineffectual in the long run. This being the case,
improvement in police-minority relations can best be obtained through refashioning the position of minority people
so that they can accept the role of the police as majority

society does. The conditions of their lives must be molded so as to transform their perceptions and attitudes until they become compatible with the perspectives of Dominant society and with the directives Dominant society enjoins upon the police.

A solution of this kind cannot be achieved cheaply or quickly. It involves making fundamental changes in entire modes of existence for millions of people. However ambitious this policy may seem, it is naive to expect that any program less far-reaching can more than paper-over the problems of the police and minorities. Often people speak as if substantial improvement in police-minority relations can be achieved more easily. Some people suggest, for example, that education can produce more harmonious relations. Policemen can be taught to be more tolerant, minority group individuals to be more understanding of the requirements of an ordered society. Education is seen as a lever that can regenerate perspectives. Education may, it is true, widen perspectives and affect behavior. But it cannot realistically be expected to permit individuals to transcend completely the demands of their social positions—whether it be that of policemen, bound by duty and desiring career success, or of the minority individual, often ill-equipped to compete in the modern world and frustrated in his attempts to achieve a position commensurate with his aspirations. Education may provide a means by which minority people can shed the worst vestiges of their deprivation. It is an avenue of upward social mobility. But for those masses of people for whom it does not become a ticket to middle-class status, education cannot be expected to override the constraints of chronically disadvantaged circumstances.

Another diagnosis frequently heard of the police-community problem is that there has been a "breakdown of communications." The problem, we are told, is that people on both sides no longer listen to one another and consequently do not get to know the problems of the other. The solution suggested is that tension can be reduced through discussion. This is an empty and impractical suggestion. Communications have indeed broken down, but the very reasons that have led to this rupture reduce the chances that further talk can be fruitful. Talk is cheap, however, and so it has an immediate appeal. Educators and scholars seem particularly fond of it. If our analysis of the roots of police-minority hostility is correct, it is exceedingly doubtful whether talk alone can solve the problem. Social reform may be assisted by talking, but talk cannot substitute for social reform.

An analysis of police-minority relations that finds the basis of the problem in the social roles and positions of both sides would seem to imply that there is very little policemen can do on their own to ameliorate the situation. This conclusion is true in part, but it should not be overdrawn. It *is* doubtful that the police can radically transform minority feelings toward them, at least in the near future, by their own unaided efforts. At the same time, policemen are an important component in the minority world; they are, as we have seen, a symbol of subordinate status. If policemen themselves can demonstrate a capacity for sympathy, understanding, and impartiality, they may begin to melt the edge of minority bitterness toward majority society. They can begin to serve as visible proof—indeed, perhaps the most visible proof—that majority society is capable of treating minority individuals in a new manner. The behavior of policemen, then, can clothe in human form the persistent, impersonal patterns of treatment directed by Dominants toward minorities. The police are in a position to engage in image-formation, for they stand for the majority community in the eyes of many minority people. While it is unlikely that policemen, however heroic their efforts, can offset the corroding effects of structural discrimination, their role has pedagogical importance because what they do will be read as proof of how majority society intends to treat minority people.

The burden of improving police-minority relations does not belong exclusively to the police. Policemen should not be expected to solve, through their own actions, the accumulated problems of generations of inequality and deprivation. Reformers of police-minority relations must beware of making the police a scapegoat for deep-seated patterns of discrimination. The police must indeed be malleable and creative; these are new times and policemen are naive if they believe that business can be done as usual. A measure of initiative certainly belongs to them. At the same time, they are creatures of the society in which they live and work. Unless that society is willing to inaugurate changes in patterns of living that touch everyone—Dominants as well as minorities—policemen will remain locked with minorities in a relationship of antagonism which neither created but from which neither can escape.

Index